JOSHUA

THE HEBREW AND GREEK TEXTS

JOSHUA

THE HEBREW AND GREEK TEXTS

by

S. HOLMES, M.A.

Lecturer in Theology, Jesus College, Oxford, and formerly
Senior Kennicott Scholar

Cambridge:
at the University Press
1914

CAMBRIDGE
UNIVERSITY PRESS

University Printing House, Cambridge CB2 8BS, United Kingdom

Published in the United States of America by Cambridge University Press, New York

Cambridge University Press is part of the University of Cambridge.

It furthers the University's mission by disseminating knowledge in the pursuit of education, learning and research at the highest international levels of excellence.

www.cambridge.org
Information on this title: www.cambridge.org/9781107697232

First published 1914
First paperback edition 2014

A catalogue record for this publication is available from the British Library

ISBN 978-1-107-69723-2 Paperback

PREFATORY NOTE

The following books have been consulted:

Hollenberg. *Der Charakter der alex. Uebersetzung des B. Josua*, 1876.

Dillmann. Commentary, 1886.

Wellhausen. *Die Comp. des Hex.* 3rd ed., 1899.

Bennett in S. B. O. T., 1895; translation and notes, 1899.

Steuernagel. Commentary, 1899.

Carpenter and Battersby. *The Hexateuch*, 2 vols., 1900.

Holzinger. Commentary, 1901.

Driver. 'Joshua' in Kittel's *Biblia Hebraica*, 1905.

Holmes and Parsons' edition of LXX. Vol. II, 1818.

Swete's Manual edition of LXX. 2nd ed., 1895.

Lucian's recension of LXX by Lagarde, 1883.

Field's *Hexapla of Origen*, 1875.

Lyons Heptateuch, i.e. The old Latin or 'Itala.' Ed. by Robert (second part), 1900.

Vulgate. Heyse and Tischendorf, 1873.

Ehrlich. *Randglossen zur Hebr. Bibel*, vol. III, 1910.

Driver. *Hebrew Text of the books of Samuel*. 2nd ed., 1913.

I have to thank Dr Driver very cordially for his kindness in finding time to look over the proofs. In accordance with his suggestion, all accents in proper names transliterated from the Hebrew have been omitted.

S. H.

JESUS COLLEGE, OXFORD.
January, 1914.

INDEX

ADDENDA AND CORRIGENDA

p. 17, l. 18. The emendation in Kittel is due to Steuernagel.

p. 19, l. 22. *After* "no other example of this meaning is known" *add* 'the passages quoted by Dillmann from Ex. x. 29, Num. xxvii. 7, xxxvi. 5 are not parallel.'

p. 32, l. 5. *Before* LXX *insert* '*v.* 13.'

p. 32, l. 25. *Add* On LXX translation 'surround' not 'march round,' see detached note, p. 37.

p. 45, viii. 31. For mistake of LXX here, cf. note on xxii. 27.

p. 52, l. 18. *Read the plural* 'These may be additions,' etc.

p. 67, *vv.* 6–10, l. 3. The waws in both cases should be disjoined from the preceding words.

p. 80, l. 1. *Read* לִפְנֵי.

INTRODUCTION

An exhaustive investigation of the Hebrew and Greek texts of the book of Joshua has not been undertaken since Hollenberg's attempt in 1876. The result of Hollenberg's enquiry was in many passages favourable to the LXX; he strongly denies deliberate alteration (p. 9), but on the whole seems to uphold the general superiority of the M. T.

Ten years later a far less favourable attitude was adopted by the great scholar Dillmann in his commentary on Joshua in 1886; he affirms that the value of LXX, in this book as well as in others, has been much overestimated. At the end of his work, p. 690, Dillmann gives his reasons for preferring in all important points the M. T. He adduces a series of passages where he alleges that alteration on the part of the LXX scribe is indubitable. The superiority of M. T. in these passages is therefore certain, and carries with it the superiority of the same text in several other passages which Dillmann admits would otherwise be doubtful. These conclusions which are accepted on the whole by Bennett (1895) are rejected by Steuernagel in his commentary on Joshua (1899). But Carpenter and H. Battersby (1900) adhere to Dillmann's general position (see vol. II. p. 319); while Holzinger (1901) explicitly affirms that the statement of Dillmann—that LXX does not offer a more original text, but represents in many cases a deliberate endeavour to avoid difficulties,—still holds good (see p. xv).

The thesis which is here offered dissents from this position. It is believed that some distinctly fresh reasons can be offered in favour of the superiority of the LXX in:

(1) The phenomenon of double and sometimes more frequent omission of the same word or expression in LXX in a large number of passages. This occurs too often to be accidental.

(2) The circumstance that in several cases where the two texts vary from one another, each text is consistent with itself; thus suggesting the hypothesis of a deliberate and systematic revision. Such systematic revision cannot be ascribed with any probability to the Greek translator and must therefore be the work of a subsequent Hebrew scribe[1].

(3) The fact that the confused LXX passage, ch. v. *vv.* 4 f., when turned back into Hebrew requires only a slight emendation to give an intelligible text manifestly earlier than M. T.

Further, the examination of Dillmann's series of 'entschieden fehlerhaft' passages which is undertaken in this thesis, shows his contention, that they undoubtedly represent deliberate alterations by the LXX, to be open to serious criticism.

Finally, on the assumption that the whole book was translated by one and the same scribe, it must be pointed out that if Dillmann's and Holzinger's position were correct we should have a translator who displays great skill in redaction in ch. xix., a conspicuous want of it in ch. vi., a keen eye for what is necessary for consistency in chs. v. and xviii., a dull perception when obvious contradictions are concerned as in ch. vi. 7, 8, 9 and 13 and ch. vii. 15 and 25. (See especially note on ch. xix. 48.)

I. The superiority, then, of LXX to M. T. is upheld by the noteworthy circumstance that in a large number of passages there occurs the repeated absence or omission of the same expression in different parts of the same narrative. In spite of the fact that Hebrew revision is fairly certain in large parts of the Old Testament, it is usual to put down to accident omissions that cannot be definitely accounted for. But when a second or third omission of the word or expression occurs later on in the same passage, it is difficult to avoid the conclusion that we have no longer to deal with the result of accident, but with either deliberate omission or deliberate insertion: i.e. with revision of the text.

The question then arises—to whom is the revision due? To a translator who, combining the functions of translator and reviser, deliberately omitted the words? or to a Hebrew reviser

[1] As against systematic revision of LXX as suggested by Holzinger see note on xxi. 42.

who deliberately inserted them? The hypothesis of deliberate omission on the part of the translator is difficult to uphold. The only reason for omission in most cases would be a desire to shorten labour; but in face of the tendency of all LXX scribes to amplify, this is improbable. Indeed our translator amplifies even where one might expect abbreviation: e.g. in chapter iii. where the oft-repeated expression "the ark of the covenant of J." lends itself to abbreviation, the translator shortens nowhere and amplifies at least in two places (see note on iii. 11).

Thus the hypothesis of shortening the text to avoid labour falls to the ground. The hypothesis of omission for the purpose of avoiding difficulties will not hold with regard to the greater part of the double omissions quoted below: at any rate with regard to the shorter phrases. Bearing in mind the style of Hebrew revision (Robertson Smith, *O. T. J. C.*[2], pp. 78 and 124) we should naturally infer that a short insertion at one point, and the repetition of such short insertion in an appropriate place later on, display the work of a Hebrew reviser who imagined he was improving the text, rather than that of a LXX translator who omitted the words for no discoverable reason.

The following are the passages where repeated omission occurs.

1. In chapter ii. *v.* 17 and *v.* 20 the spies say to Rahab "We will be guiltless of the oath which thou hast caused us to swear."

The two Hebrew words translated "which thou hast caused us to swear" are not represented in the Greek of either *v.* 17 or *v.* 20. Even if the words on their first occurrence in *v.* 17 were omitted by accident it would be very strange if the same accident occurred again a few lines later on in *v.* 20. It can be proved moreover that the translator in this passage was under no desire to shorten the text, for in *v.* 19 to the words "and we will be guiltless" he makes an addition by inserting the words "of this thy oath." This addition which is in accordance with the LXX tendency of amplification makes it difficult to believe that the same writer deliberately omitted the words "which thou hast caused us to swear," in *v.* 17 and again in *v.* 20.

2. v. 11 and 12. Here the expression ממחרת is omitted in both verses. The expression does not occur again in Joshua, so

it is possible to argue that the translator was ignorant of its meaning (so Hollenberg), but against this must be set the fact that in the six or seven places where the word occurs in the Pentateuch it is rightly translated.

3. In vi. 4 and 6 the words "and seven priests shall carry seven trumpets of rams' horns before the ark" are absent in both places.

4. In chapter viii. the passage where the battle before Ai is narrated, the same expression is absent from the Greek three times. In two LXX verses, 15 and 20, there is no reference to "the wilderness" mentioned in the Hebrew as the direction in which the Israelites fled; and in *v.* 24 the wilderness is mentioned again in M. T. and is again absent from the LXX. This however is not a triple but a double 'omission,' as המדבר in 24 is a corruption of המורד (LXX κατάβασις).

5. In chapter x. *v.* 15 after the Battle of Beth Horon we read: "and Joshua returned, and all Israel with him, unto the camp at Gilgal." At the end of the chapter, *v.* 43, the same words occur. In both cases the clause is absent from the LXX. With regard to *v.* 15 Bennett affirms it to be omitted by the Greek translator in order to avoid contradiction with a later verse, *v.* 21, where Joshua is found at Makkedah. This is the view also of Holzinger. It postulates that the translator was also a reviser and looked ahead; but what probability it has is seriously diminished by the fact that the same words in *v.* 43, the last verse in the chapter, are omitted also. All scholars agree that *v.* 42 is the close of a section. Even a very dull scribe could see that the clause in question is in an appropriate place in *v.* 43. Our own division of the chapter shows that. No reason whatever can be alleged for the second omission of the words except the simple one that they were not in the text used by the translator. But if the clause is an insertion of the Hebrew reviser in *v.* 43 it is most probably his insertion in *v.* 15 also.

6. In chapter x. the phrase "great stones" occurs in verses 11, 18 and 27 of the Hebrew. In each case the adjective 'great' is absent from the LXX. Had the reverse been the case no one would have doubted that the additional word was inserted by the Greek translator in accordance with the usual tendency to amplify. That tendency to amplify makes it

almost certain that the adjective 'great' was not in the original text. (גדלות in *v.* 11 may be a deviation and not an insertion. See note.)

7. In x. 24 LXX omits המלכים האלה twice.

8. In chapter xix. there is a sixfold omission of למשפחתם and a fourfold omission of מטה. See note on xix. 1.

9. In 16 b and 31 b the double absence of the article and demonstrative (= these) cannot be ascribed to accident.

10. In *vv.* 15, 22 and 30, 38 and 39 the repeated absence of the b clauses in LXX (so many cities and their villages) points to subsequent amplification in the Hebrew. This is confirmed by the fact that in the 10 places in ch. xv. where similar clauses occur they are duly rendered.

11. In xxi. 5, 6, 7 (taking M. T. as generally emended) we find that the LXX omits למשפחתם in *vv.* 5 and 6 and renders it in *v.* 7. This points to the conclusion that *vv.* 5 and 6 did not originally contain the expression, but were afterwards assimilated to *v.* 7. It is most unlikely that a translator would look ahead, and notice the same expression in three verses, omit the expression in the first two verses and render it in the third. If the omission were deliberate a reverse process would have taken place.

Compare also vi. 7 and 13 and vii. 6, triple omission of ארון, vi. 19 and 24, double omission of וכלי, viii. 9 b and 13, of וילן, viii. 31 and 34 of "the book" in the phrase "the book of the law," xii. 9 to 24 the omission of אחד 29 or 30 times, xxii. 31 and 32 double omission of "son of Eleazar."

In x. 22 and 23 the omission of אלי and אליו and in *vv.* 22 and 27 of את פי before "the cave" may be instances of abbreviation. Something similar to double omission occurs in ii. 14 and 18 and xviii. 6 and 8 where instances of double deviation occur; see notes.

In addition to the repeated omission of the same phrase in close juxtaposition, there are also instances of it at wider intervals spread over the whole book. The omission of geographical details in i. 14, v. 1, 10, vii. 2, 5, xiii. 22, xvi. 1, xvii. 5, xviii. 18, 19, xx. 8, xxi. 21 and xxiv. 3 seems to point to subsequent revision and insertion in the Hebrew rather than deliberate omission by LXX.

ויאמר which is found 53 times in M. T. is absent from LXX in iii. 10, iv. 21, vii. 2, x. 24 and xxii. 8. The last is certainly an addition subsequent to LXX, in each of the other four cases there is something to be said for the Greek.

Lastly לאמר, which occurs 43 times in M. T., is absent from LXX four times, i. 13, iii. 6, iv. 3 and iv. 22. Here, very strong evidence indeed can be adduced in support of the faithfulness of LXX in two of these places. The Hebrew writers did not always insert לאמר after ויאמר; this seems to have been the case especially where a command follows, see iii. 5, 9, iv. 5, vi. 7, vii. 19, x. 18. In all these passages ויאמר is followed by a command and לאמר is not used. Now it is worth noticing that in i. 13 and iii. 6 according to LXX an imperative follows ויאמר without the intervention of לאמר, and on the analogy of iii. 5 etc. this construction is quite probable. As to the other two instances, iv. 3 as shown in the note has almost certainly suffered from the hand of the reviser, and it also may be pointed out that *v.* 16 in the same chapter has the imperative of צוה without לאמר following as would be the case in *v.* 3 if LXX were right. In iv. 22 it is possible that לאמר was omitted by LXX. It is the third repetition of the word in two lines, and the translator may excusably have dropped it and substituted ὅτι, yet in the parallel passage in *v.* 7 ואמרתם which corresponds to והודעתם is not followed by לאמר. It is surely favourable to the general faithfulness of LXX that in an expression which lends itself to omission, 39 instances are duly rendered out of 43, while of the four omissions two are probably right, one is excusable, and as to the fourth (iv. 3), the fact that the deviation of the texts is not confined to the omission of לאמר leaves the matter in suspense.

It may also be here noticed that in some passages where two similar expressions occur in the Hebrew the LXX omits the first expression and translates the second. Had the translator been a reviser he would have reversed this method of procedure: he would have translated the phrase when it first came before him and omitted the repetition. These may be called "anticipatory" insertions. See i. 14 and 15, ii. 9 and 24, 14 and 20, iii. 13 and 16, iv. 3 and 9, viii. 8 and 19, ix. 21 and 27, x. 37 and 39 "its king and its cities." Where, as in vi. 25, xii. 6 and xxii. 5, the second occurrence of a phrase is omitted, it is impossible to say what the original text had.

II. The second point which tells in favour of the originality of the LXX is the consistency which obtains in many of its deviations from M. T. The following are the passages where this consistency is found: v. 8, vi. 8, x. 28, xvi. 3, 10, xviii. 2—10, xx. 3, xxii. 8.

In chapter v. where the circumcision of the Israelites at Gilgal is narrated, M. T. v. 8 reads "And it came to pass when they had finished circumcising כל הגוי they abode" etc., while the LXX gives περιτμηθέντες which is a neat rendering of the whole clause minus כל הגוי. The omission of כל הגוי is most unlike a LXX translator; the love of amplification which is noticeable all through LXX, including this book, is distinctly against it. In addition, the reading is consistent with the rest of LXX text which does not recognise the circumcision of the whole nation, and thus goes to support the contention that the translator rendered his text faithfully. This passage is further discussed below on p. 9 and in the notes.

In chapter vi. 8 the M. T. gives *the* seven priests, while the article is wanting in LXX. This is consistent with the fact that we have here the first mention of priests in LXX. A mere abbreviator, and an unskilful one at that if Dillmann's position is right, would hardly have been keen enough to drop the ה in הכהנים in order to remove any trace of his earlier omission of the word.

In chapter x. 28, 30, 35, 37, M. T. reads כל הנפש and LXX offers πᾶν ἐμπνέον = כל הנשמה. In *v.* 40 however M. T. gives כל הנשמה and LXX as before πᾶν ἐμπνέον. The conclusion seems certain that the LXX read in every place כל הנשמה and that the Hebrew reviser, being of the same opinion as Dillmann on Deuteronomy ch. xx. 16 that the word נשמה applies to human beings only, altered הנשמה into הנפש in the first four places. But *v.* 40 escaped to turn what would otherwise have been a probability into a certainty. See Carpenter and Battersby *in loco.*

In xvi. 3 the M. T. וירד upholds the LXX reading in *v.* 1 which would be ועלה.

xvi. 10, see note.

xviii. 1—10. It is generally agreed that *vv.* 2—10 (except 7) belong to the older narrative and have no connection with *v.* 1 which states that the whole congregation assembled themselves together at Shiloh. In *vv.* 2—10 the Israelites are not at Shiloh but perhaps as Steuernagel suggests at Gilgal. The differences in the two texts in the light of this fact strongly support the superiority of the LXX. The Hebrew reviser made certain alterations under the impression that the scene of action was at Shiloh the well-known sanctuary. In *v.* 6 according to the true reading of the LXX (see note) Joshua says "bring it (the survey of the land) to me, and I will cast lots before Jahveh." Under the impression that Joshua was at Shiloh the Hebrew reviser inserted the word 'here,' "and I will cast lots here before Jahveh." In *v.* 8 the LXX A has "come to me here and I will cast lots." The Hebrew reviser made another alteration similar to the first and wrote "return to me and here will I cast lots." Further, still under the influence of *v.* 1, he adds to *v.* 9 "to the camp at Shiloh" (not in LXX), and to *v.* 10 "and there Joshua divided the land." The old narrative was worked over to bring it into harmony with the new introduction. The LXX 2—10 is consistent with a scene of action other than Shiloh, the M. T. is consistent if 1—10 be taken as a whole. Revision, and very careful revision, of the Hebrew text seems undeniable here.

In chapter xx. the Deuteronomic expression בלי דעת is omitted in *v.* 3, consistently with the omission of the Deuteronomic verses 4, 5, and 6.

xxii. 8. The omission of ויאמר אליהם is consistently followed by "And they returned," not by a speech as in M. T., and וישובו is consistently omitted at the beginning of *v.* 9.

It must however be mentioned that in chapter xxiv. the LXX has a double variation which is consistent and wrong. The translation substitutes Shiloh for Shechem in *v.* 1, and repeats the substitution in *v.* 25. Here the LXX reading is unanimously rejected; no reason can be adduced why M. T. should make any alteration. But a very good reason can be discovered for the alteration by LXX. Shiloh was well known as a sanctuary from the first book of Samuel, from Jeremiah and from Psalm lxxviii. 61, whereas the sanctity of Shechem can only be inferred from incidental notices. The LXX translator made the alteration influenced by the fact that Shiloh was known to him as a celebrated sanctuary of early times and moreover is the only sanctuary so far mentioned in Joshua. Six times in the last few chapters Shiloh is mentioned as the sanctuary. The statement of Bennett that the substitution is a harmonistic alteration with reference to chapter xviii. is imperfect. It is a harmonistic alteration with reference to xviii. 1, 10; xix. 37; xxi. 2; xxii. 9, 12. (In xviii. 8 Shiloh is not in LXX.) With Shiloh in his head as the sacred place the Greek translator made his only important deliberate alteration. It is an alteration of the same nature as that of "men" into "princes" which he made in the narrative of the Gibeonites. It is simple and induced by the context.

The difference between this and the other instances, especially the one in chapter xviii., lies in the fact that a good and simple reason can be given for LXX alteration here. In chapter xviii. there is a reason for the M. T. alteration, none for LXX: in chapter xxiv. there is a reason for the LXX alteration, none for M. T. There is another consistent and perhaps wrong alteration in xv. 1; xvi. 1 and xvii. 1: see note on xv. 1.

III. The third point in favour of the superiority of the LXX text is to be found in the passage, ch. v. *vv.* 4 f., which by a slight emendation can be cleared of Hollenberg's charge of being "geradezu unsinnig und voller Widersprüche" (p. 18).

By this emendation a narrative can be educed, which is in one respect more consistent than M. T. with the sentence "This day have I rolled away the reproach of Egypt from off you." As shown in the note, the passage as emended runs thus: "And this was the manner in which Joshua circumcised the children of Israel. All those who were born by the way, *and all those who were uncircumcised of them that came up out of Egypt*, all these did Joshua circumcise. For the children of Israel had wandered forty years in the wilderness, therefore uncircumcised were most of them. As for the men of war, who came up out of Egypt, who did not obey the voice of Jahveh, he had sworn to them that he would not let them see, etc." This text was revised from a religious standpoint. The Reviser's overworking here and his omissions in xxi. 42 d and xxiv. 30 a, where the mention of the 'flint knives' would have called to mind the circumcision at Gilgal, are all due to the same motive. If the LXX text is original the Hebrew reviser would have the strongest motive for alteration: he would be most reluctant to admit that any of the Israelites in Egypt were uncircumcised. On the other hand the hypothesis of deliberate alteration from M. T. seems hopeless. The LXX translator could not possibly have gone out of his way to make a statement which implied that the Israelites did not universally practise circumcision while in Egypt. If probability is to be any guide it must be admitted that LXX here had a very different text from ours and one that was earlier in point of time. Holzinger admits the existence of additions in M. T., but reference to the notes will show that the whole passage has been recast.

We now come to the consideration of those passages where Dillmann thinks that alteration by LXX is certain. As already mentioned his argument is, that if one considers ii. 15 b; vi. 3—5; vii. 17, 25; viii. 9 b, 11 b, 12—18, 20, 26; x. 13, 15, 37, 43; xiii. 29; xiv. 3; xviii. 10; xxii. 11, to be purposely abbreviated, then ii. 15; v. 4—7; viii. 7 f.; xxiii. 16; xxiv. 5, which are in themselves doubtful, must also be considered instances of deliberate alteration.

Yet when the passages in the first series are discussed one by one, it is impossible to admit the certainty which Dillmann affirms. In ii. 15, the passage localises the house of Rahab; and its position is so firmly fixed in the minds of modern readers that it seems inconceivable that the words were not always in the text; but no satisfactory reason can be offered for the omission of them by LXX if they were before the translator. Moreover Jerome's rendering "domus enim ejus haerebat muro" seems to show that he had not the full reading of our present Hebrew text before him, a circumstance which confirms Steuernagel's suggestion that the passage in M. T. consists of two variants. Hollenberg (p. 18) considers the passage to be a late explanation, and Carpenter and Battersby, who on the whole adopt Dillmann's position, here say "the clauses describing the situation of Rahab's house seem explanatory insertions." Holzinger however affirms the omission to be intentional: if the house had been on the wall it would be destroyed when the walls of the town were overthrown. Here again one must demur to the supposition that the translator can be credited with the power of detecting inconsistencies, which are not of the plainest character.

Generations of readers have heard of the position of Rahab's house without seeing the difficulty: it is to be doubted whether the LXX translator would be any more critical. In view of the fact that Hollenberg, Carpenter and Battersby, as well as Steuernagel, prefer the LXX we must dismiss this passage from the number of those where deliberate abbreviation is certain.

vi. 3 b and c, and 4. It is not easy to see why these verses should have been omitted if they were before the LXX translator. It could not be for the purpose of avoiding difficulties, for there are none. But the verses cannot be considered apart from the rest of the chapter. Dillmann, Bennett, Carpenter and Battersby, all consider that LXX shortened the text of ch. vi. to avoid the difficulties in the Hebrew.

Now the difficulties in the early part of the chapter are threefold:

(1) In *v.* 5 the shout which is to bring down the walls is to follow a blast on the trumpet. In *v.* 10 it is to follow Joshua's command to shout.

(2) The question how a single blast could be the signal for the shout when the seven priests are said to be continually blowing with the trumpets during the whole circuit.

(3) The strange circumstance that a rearguard is represented as blowing horns on the march at the same time as the priests.

The first and second difficulties remain in the LXX, the third also is found in *v.* 9: its absence in *v.* 13 as we now have it is due to accidental omission, which was followed by corruption of the text (see note).

Therefore all three difficulties are found in LXX. But further it must be noticed that the LXX has additional difficulties of its own. If we examine the Greek text we find the narrative of the order of the procession hopelessly inconsistent. In *v.* 7 the armed men are to march in front of the ark; in *v.* 8 the seven priests march in front of the ark; in *v.* 9 we have the armed men first, then the ark, and then the priests, or perhaps a rearguard, behind the ark; i.e. in three consecutive verses the procession is arranged in three different ways[1].

These inconsistencies, it is here suggested, were in the Hebrew text before the Greek translator and were subsequently dealt with by a Hebrew reviser. They were very plain and called for a remedy. This remedy was supplied first by an insertion at the very beginning of the narrative, where in *v.* 4 M. T. Jahveh directs that seven priests are to go before the

[1] It is possible to put the contradictions in a less glaring way by saying that in *vv.* 7 and 8 the armed men and the seven priests are both to go before the ark though their relative positions are not defined, and that in *v.* 9 as emended though the seven priests who are to go before the ark are not mentioned explicitly, yet they are referred to in the suffix supplied by conjecture. In *v.* 13 as emended the order corresponds with that of M. T. See notes.

ark. Secondly by an addition to *v.* 6 in which Joshua repeats the command that seven priests are to go before the ark.

Thus in the Hebrew text with the two commands and the execution of the commands in 8 and 13, there are four statements as to the position of the seven priests before the ark. There remains one statement in *v.* 7 Hebrew, that the armed men are to go before the ark, but this even if noticed only puzzles the reader for a moment; two verses later on it is explained by the words (which do not agree with the LXX) "the armed men went before the priests."

As to the relative perspicuity of these two texts we have a very unprejudiced witness. Hollenberg writing in 1876 said "The M.T. has only in *v.* 8 one difficulty, where it is said 'when Joshua had spoken to the people' when he had not previously spoken to them at all" (p. 18). I.e. the revision has been so skilfully done that a competent modern scholar in 1876 could find very little fault with it. Are we to believe that where Hollenberg could detect no particular difficulties, the LXX translator could? The reason given for regarding the LXX text as an abbreviation of the M. T., viz. the desire to avoid difficulties, requires us to believe that the translator could see difficulties which a critical scholar of the present day did not see; and indeed that in his endeavours to avoid them he produced a narrative which contains all the original difficulties with others in addition.

On the other hand good reasons can be given for the insertions and alterations in the M. T. The Revisers found the text in a state of confusion in regard to the order of the procession. Alterations had to be made, the exact position of the armed men and the seven priests had to be settled, and the very ingenious device was adopted of telling the reader at the beginning what order to expect: later on the order was emphasised by repetition. The hypothesis of revision by a Hebrew editor seems to give the only reasonable account of the phenomena in this chapter.

In vii. 17—18, the longest omission might be due to homoioteleuton. The eye of the scribe might have passed from ויקרב of *v.* 17 to the same word at the beginning of *v.* 18. But a reference to the note will show that there is considerable probability of LXX being right.

In verse 25 the problem is very complicated. In *v.* 15 punishment by fire is threatened; and it is natural to assume that the threat would be carried out and recorded in *v.* 25. Supposing M. T. (they stoned him, they burnt them, they stoned them) to be before the translator, he simplified inconsistently. He should have omitted the stoning and retained the burning. He omitted the burning and retained the stoning. This being so, it is a case which proves the want of ability on the part of the translator to detect inconsistencies at any distance from one another. He shortened the phrase before him: it is alleged he did so, because it seemed inconsistent in itself; and yet he retained the part that was inconsistent with *v.* 15. There is no desire to place too much stress upon this, as the matter is far from simple; but this much is certain, *v.* 25 in LXX is still inconsistent with *v.* 15, in spite of the alleged alteration made to obtain consistency.

Dillmann's references to chapter viii. (the capture of Ai) are 9b, 11b, 12—18, 20, 26. Now 9 b and 13 b stand or fall together (see note). The omission of the passage after העיר in *v.* 11, to לעיר in *v.* 13, may be explained by homoioteleuton: *v.* 20 refers to the flight to the wilderness, and as shown in the note on 15 b is almost certainly the addition of a Hebrew reviser; *v.* 26 if genuine might possibly have been omitted by homoioteleuton, but see the note on *v.* 18.

With regard to *vv.* 12—18 it must be admitted that the LXX narrative is free from the discrepancy of the numbers of the men in ambush; and one cannot help thinking that this has been the main reason why scholars have assented to the alleged inferiority of the Greek text. Certainly if the translator did deliberately omit the verses it would cast suspicion on some at any rate of the other passages where the Greek differs from the Hebrew text. Yet against the theory of deliberate omission the following suggestions seem worth considering. If the translator had felt the difficulty there was open to him the simple expedient of making the numbers correspond. A translator who could omit several words to avoid a difficulty, was equally capable of altering a single number for the same end. Moreover the contention that these verses were omitted on account of the contradiction, would be more convincing if the verse containing it were the only one wanting in the Greek text at this point. In addition to *v.* 12, 11 b and the greater part of 13 are omitted; without necessity if the theory of deliberate omission be true. Again, the theory of deliberate omission from the text as we now have it ascribes to the translator a performance which seems too ingenious to be true. According to this hypothesis the Greek translator first passed over 29 or 30 words. Then he took the next three words and translated them. Then he omitted the next six words, and afterwards went on with the narrative; i.e. a long piece was omitted, a short piece was translated, and a second short piece omitted. This would be a strange performance, but it is what must have been done if the translator had our M. T. before him.

The problem presented by ch. viii. is no doubt troublesome. The original Hebrew text may have been the same as the present LXX text; or it may have been longer than the LXX but shorter than our present Hebrew text. But it is hardly possible that the Hebrew before the LXX was the same as ours.

x. 13 omits the celebrated phrase, "Is it not written in the book of Jasher?" but Mr Thackeray, *J. T. S.* vol. XI. p. 528, gives reasons for thinking it was not in the text. That in *v.* 37 LXX omitted "the king thereof" because the death of the king of Hebron was already recorded in verse 26, is not likely from what we know of the translator. Indeed it rather comes under the head of 'double omission,' see *v.* 28, where the same phrase is absent from LXX. Verses 15 and 43 are discussed above, p. 4.

xiii. 29. This may be an instance of omission by design, and if so a very excusable one, but it may have been caused by homoioteleuton. But see note on xix. 1.

xiv. 3. Could be omission by homoioteleuton.

xviii. 10. Ascribed by Dillmann himself to the hand of a Redactor.

xxii. 11. Probably the misreading of a difficult phrase.

Having discussed the passages where the LXX gives the shorter text Dillmann objects to those where the Greek text is longer than the Hebrew, viz. viii. 18, ix. 27, x. 12, xiii. 7, xx. 3, xxiii. 5, xxiv. 4. These passages are dealt with in the notes.

In addition he maintains that vi. 26, xvi. 10, xix. 48, xxi. 42, xxiv. 33 are entirely derived from other books. These passages are also discussed in the notes, but it may be well to follow Dillmann's plan and take a crucial instance first. Such an instance may be found in xix. 47. Part of Josh. xix. 47 LXX is not in the M. T. and corresponds to Judges i. 34, 35 M. T. and LXX. The text in parallel columns will enable the argument to be more easily followed.

HEBREW TEXT

47 And the border of the sons of Dan was too narrow[1] for them, and the sons of Dan went up and fought with Leshem, and took it, and smote it according to the mouth of the sword and took possession of it, and dwelt in it, and called Leshem, Dan, according to the name of Dan their father.

48 This is the inheritance of the tribe of the sons of Dan according to their families: these cities and their villages.

LXX

48 This is the inheritance of the tribe of the sons of Dan, according to their families, their cities and their villages.

a. And the sons of Dan did not drive out the Amorite, who drove them into the hill country, and the Amorite did not allow them to come down into the valley | 47 and made narrow for them the border of their district.

b. And the sons of Judah went forth and fought against Lachish and took it and smote it with the mouth of the sword, and dwelt in it, and called the name of it Lasendak.

c. And the Amorite continued[2] to dwell in Elom and in Salamein, and the hand of Ephraim was heavy upon them, and they became tributary to them.

If we assume the LXX to represent the original, the way in which our Hebrew text arose is fairly simple. The original contained an extract from P winding up with the usual subscription, "This is the inheritance of the tribe of the children of Dan," etc. Then came an extract from J consisting of three sections; *a*, which describes the failure of the Danites to maintain their place in the South, *b* which describes their subsequent victory in the North, and *c* which states that the Amorites continue to dwell in Elom. The Hebrew reviser objected to any mention of the failure of Dan and consequently omitted it, as well as the section which relates that the Amorites continued to dwell in Elom. The section containing the account of the conquest of Laish by Dan he

[1] A generally accepted emendation.

[2] ὑπέμεινεν.

retained but transferred it to a position before P's subscription. This is a perfectly simple and intelligible proceeding; omission of unsatisfactory details, retention of satisfactory details, the whole being rounded off.

If on the contrary it is maintained that our present Hebrew text is the original, then the LXX translator must have set to work as follows. He must have cleverly picked out the P subscription and put it in the right place at the end of the P section. Then instead of simply adding the narrative from Judges to the Joshua narrative before him, he recast it in excellent order—the failure of the Danites, the subsequent conquest of Laish by the Danites and then the less important statement that the Amorites continued to dwell in Elom until they were subdued by Ephraim. He leaves the passage in perfect order just as the writer of the oldest book might have penned it. It seems incredible that such a skilful performance as this could come from the hand of our translator. His was the humbler task of simply translating the original: the section of P and the section of J as they appeared in his Hebrew text.

Further, the use of ὑπομένω (continue) in *c* seems decisive for a Hebrew original. The meaning of the word הואיל was not known to the Greek translators. In the passage in Judges and in Josh. xvii. 12 it is rendered by ἄρχομαι: in Josh. vii. 7 by καταμένω. The only possible inference is that the translator had a Hebrew text before him: that ὑπέμεινεν is his rendering of ויואל and not an inexplicable variant of ἤρξατο in Judges i. 35.

A final argument for the superiority of the LXX may be found in the recent suggestion that the translation was the work of two hands, which if correct will partially invalidate the argument on p. 2, l. 14, but perhaps gives more than it takes away. Mr Thackeray in his *Grammar of O. T. Gk*, pp. viii and 13, affirms the existence of two translators of Joshua, and if one may judge from the renderings of 'Lebanon' in the book, the division took place at ch. x. or xi., for we get Ἀντιλίβανος in i. 4 and ix. 1 while in xi. 17; xii. 7; xiii. 5, 6, the form Λίβανος is used. But the fact that in both parts of the book considerable differences from M. T. occur, strengthens the conclusion that the translators had an original before them different from the present Hebrew text.

CHAPTER I.

1. נון. LXX Ναυη, i.e. NAYH for NAYN, see Swete, *Introduction to O. T. in Gk*, p. 480 note 2. In the ancient characters N and H were frequently confused. See Cobet's *Variae Lectiones*, p. 3. It is strange that this error should be constant.

2. The last two words לבני ישראל should be omitted with LXX. The anticipation of the object is an Aramaic rather than a Hebrew construction, though it is found in some places, see Dr Driver's full note on 1 Sam. xxi. 14. If therefore the LXX omit either the pronominal suffix or the separate object it may be presumed that they give the earlier reading. In 1 Sam. xxi. 14 and 2 Sam. xix. 6 LXX omit the suffix; here they omit the separate object.

4. מהמדבר. LXX took this and הלבנון as accusatives after נתתי in *v.* 3. Jerome had the same text as ours, for "A deserto et Libano" does not show that he read מן before הלבנון. If therefore we are to read with Holzinger מהלבנון it must be simply as a conjectural emendation.

Dr Driver in Kittel conjectures ועד הלבנון, and following Deut. xi. 24 reads מן הנהר for ועד הנהר. The reduction of ועד to ו probably took place also in xxiii. 4 והים for ועד הים and perhaps in LXX in xiii. 4, see note. When ועד had fallen out or was reduced to ו, confusion in the other prepositions would naturally follow.

כל ארץ החתים. Not in LXX or the parallel passage Deut. xi. 24. To be omitted therefore as a late insertion.

הגדול. LXX BA ἐσχάτης = האחרון. So in Deut. xi. 24. הגדול was probably an explanatory gloss, as הים האחרון occurs only four times Deut. xi. 24, xxxiv. 2, Joel ii. 20, Zech. xiv. 8.

7. Neither רק nor מאד is represented in LXX. In *v.* 18 רק is rendered by ἀλλά, but the translator may not have been consistent in the retention or omission of small words.

התורה. LXX omits. The LXX reading together with ממנו makes it almost certain that התורה is a late addition and that the original reading was simply ככל אשר. Note that in *v.* 18 לכל אשר is rendered by καθ' ὅτι.

συνῇς. LXX always misses the exact meaning of השכיל 'to prosper.' See Deut. xxix. 8 and 1 Sam. xviii. 5 with Driver's note.

תלך. LXX πράσσῃς: a deliberate alteration induced by the preceding mistake. "Thou shalt be wise in whatsoever thou doest."

8. καὶ εὐοδώσει τὰς ὁδούς σου. A doublet. Lyons Hept. with some Gk MSS rendered the doublet and omitted the original.

תשמר. LXX εἰδῇς. LXX most probably misread the word as תשכל and as this had been translated by συνῇς just before, varied with εἰδῇς.

11. לרשתה. Not in LXX. The expression must be compared with וירשתם אתה in *v.* 15 which is also absent from LXX. As pointed out in the Introduction, the fact that two similar expressions in M. T. are omitted from LXX, raises the suspicion that they are insertions by a later hand. It must however be admitted that לרשתה is used as in the text, in Deut. iii. 18, v. 31, ix. 6, xii. 1, xix. 2, 14, xxi. 1 (LXX omits in xix. 2), so that it is a phrase one would expect, and the omission here may, as in Deut. xix. 2, have been an accident.

13. יהוה אלהיכם מניח לכם ונתן. On comparing these words with Deut. iii. 18 one might be inclined to emend here with Kautzsch, who claims the authority of LXX κατέπαυσεν καὶ ἔδωκεν, and Ehrlich to הניח (and of course ונתן to ויתן), but the idea of rest which is absent from the passage in Deuteronomy makes all the difference. The writer no doubt felt that the settlement of the two and a half tribes who had still to help the others in the coming conflict, would be more rightly described by the participle indicating the future.

14. משה בעבר הירדן. Not in LXX. Probably introduced from the end of *v.* 15.

15. Read with LXX אלהיכם which dropped out of M. T. owing to its resemblance to לאחיכם.

וירשתם אותה to be omitted with LXX: so Dillmann.

עבד יהוה is omitted in i. 1, 15, xii. 6 b, xxii. 5. It is retained in i. 13, viii. 31—33, xi. 12, xii. 6 a, xiii. 8, xiv. 7, xviii. 7, xxii. 2. In xii. 6 b and xxii. 5 it may of course have been dropped by LXX as having occurred just before, but cf. viii. 31 and 33 where it is rendered.

CHAPTER II.

1. חרש. A hapax leg. not represented in LXX. Hollenberg suggests omission through ignorance of the word; but it may be due to the reviser who inserted תקוה in *v.* 18, which also occurs only in this chapter, and is not represented in the Greek. Ehrlich's suggestion to read יריחו is negatived by the usage of מרגלים: see note on vi. 23.

LXX = וילכו שני האנשים ויבאו אל יריחו ויבאו בית אשה. The 'two men' may be an explicit subject but אל יריחו ויבאו may have been in the text and omitted by homoioteleuton. τὴν Ἰεριχω after εἰς in 54, 108 and 118 is no doubt right, see note on iv. 13.

2. הלילה, not in LXX *v.* 2. It appears in *v.* 3.

3. הבאים אליך אשר באו לביתך. LXX εἰσπεπορευμένους εἰς τὴν οἰκίαν σου, omitting אליך אשר באו, Pesh. ܕܥܠܘ ܠܒܝܬܟܝ, omitting אשר באו לביתך. There is here a conflate reading. Strictly according to the evidence the conflate reading should be הבאים אליך לביתך. This represents only part of our M. T.; אשר באו may therefore be attributed to the scribe who put the two readings together.

4. שני. Absent from LXX A: where A differs from M. T. it is worth considering.

Read with LXX ותצפנם.

ותאמר כן. And she said—? Dillmann, 'richtig!' 'allerdings!' Oxford *Lexicon*, 'Right,' 'true.' Pesh. ܫܪܝܪܐܝܬ. But no other example of this meaning is known. Ehrlich's statement that it = כדבריכם כן הוא requires too much to be 'understood.' LXX has εἶπεν αὐτοῖς λέγουσα. If αὐτοῖς = להם it may give the solution of the difficulty. Taking the ל of LXX and כן of M. T. we get לכן which is used idiomatically in replies; see Oxford *Lexicon*, p. 487. The LXX seem generally to have misunderstood this idiomatic use of לכן (see *Lexicon*) and would be very likely to read להם if it would make sense. Judges xi. 8 may be compared though there the clause is suppressed which here is explicit. "True (we did drive thee out) but"—Here "true the men did come to me but."—The emendation is (1) idiomatic, (2) accounts for the ל in LXX, otherwise inexplicable, (3) does away with the necessity of postulating an unparalleled meaning for כן. Steuernagel's translation 'Jawohl' suits לכן but hardly כן.

ולא ידעתי מאין המה omitted in LXX: perhaps accidentally.

מהר omitted in LXX unless the translator thought the compound verb expressed the idea. Cf. iii. 6 προπορεύεσθε.

7. סגרו אחרי כאשר. LXX ἐκλείσθη. καὶ ἐγένετο ὡς κ.τ.λ. = סגר: ויהי כאשר. The LXX deserves the preference. For ἐκλείσθη points to סגר which is more idiomatic than סגרו. This leaves ו to be attached to the next word and gives ואחרי which καὶ ἐγένετο shows to be a corruption of ויהי. For confusion of א and ו see Zech. xi. 13: י was the same size as ו which is often confused with ר.

The adoption of the LXX reading solves the trouble about the anomalous phrase אחרי כאשר which cannot be right. Some alteration must be made if the requirements of grammar are to be satisfied. The text cannot stand as it is (though Bennett by some oversight leaves it). We must either adopt LXX ויהי כאשר, a phrase recurring in iv. 1, iv. 11, v. 8, or strike out the כ and read אחרי אשר. If we adopt אחרי אשר the אחריהם at the end of the verse is not pleasing. It must also be urged that ויהי כאשר is equivalent to a various reading, while אחרי אשר is a conjectural emendation.

Adopting LXX reading we have an exact parallel in the true text of 1 Sam. i. 12 and 13. There as here we have (1) ויהי, (2) two circumstantial clauses and (3) Imperf. with waw consec. answering ויהי. The circumstantial clauses are of course of the kind discussed in Driver, *Tenses*, § 168.

9. The last six words in M.T. are absent from LXX. Hollenberg suggests that the eye of the scribe passed from וכי to כי the first word of *v.* 10. But it is quite possible that they are an insertion from *v.* 24. Cf. *vv.* 14 and 20 and see Intro., p. 6.

11. הוא אלהים. LXX did not understand this use of הוא, see ch. xxiv. 17. B gives ὅς, representing הוא and omitting אלהים; but as ὅς and θεός were often difficult to distinguish in the MSS. it is probable that אלהים was originally represented and הוא omitted. So LXX A.

12. ונתתם לי אות אמת. Not in LXX. "Either the remainder of a fuller text or a later addition" (Dillmann). It interrupts the connection and is better away. Holzinger thinks that LXX omitted the words "aus Stilgefühl." But the translator of למען יראתם in iv. 24 had no acute feeling for Hebrew style. The phrase is probably an insertion by the Hebrew reviser to

anticipate *v.* 18 where the scarlet cord is given to Rahab by the spies. Here Rahab is made to ask for the sign which was given later on. In *v.* 18 את was already misread as אות.

13. את אחיותי. LXX = את כל ביתי. *v.* 18 b M. T. favours LXX.

14. אם לא תגידו את דברנו זה. Not in LXX. Perhaps introduced from *v.* 20. The LXX gives the following words to Rahab, "When the Lord shall have delivered the city to you." This no doubt arose from לנו being read as לכם (the confusion is frequent) and καὶ αὐτὴ εἶπεν was then inserted. Or it may be that והיה was written indistinctly and taken as ותאמר. See also in *v.* 20 "If any one harm us," first person for third.

הארץ. LXX τὴν πόλιν. Same deviation as in 18 a.

15. בחבל. Not in LXX. Perhaps omitted by accident, the next word begins with ב.

"For her house," etc. The last seven words of M. T. are not in LXX. A gloss. See Intro., p. 10.

16. After הרדפים the LXX ὀπίσω ὑμῶν perhaps represents אחריכם or rather מאחריכם. It may have fallen out from M. T. on account of its similarity to the next word ואחר.

17. אשר השבעתנו. Omitted by LXX here and in *v.* 20. A case of double 'omission.' See Intro., p. 3.

18 a. בארץ. LXX better εἰς μέρος τῆς πόλεως = בקצה העיר "into the outskirts of the city," cf. *v.* 14. Perhaps this gave rise to the tradition that Rahab's house was "on the wall."

18 b. את תקות חוט השני הזה. LXX prefixes καὶ θήσεις τὸ σημεῖον, and goes on τὸ σπαρτίον τὸ κόκκινον τοῦτο ἐκδήσεις.

Hollenberg, p. 2, regards θήσεις as a corruption of δήσεις and takes θήσεις (or δήσεις) τὸ σημεῖον as a doublet. At first sight however the genuineness of καὶ θήσεις seems guaranteed by the καὶ which might represent the waw introducing the apodosis ונתת, and אות also by the gloss in *v.* 12. But the Lyons Heptateuch has "hoc erit signum; spartum coccinum hoc deligabis in fenestram" as if it read τὸ σημεῖον τὸ σπαρτίον τὸ κόκκινον τοῦτο without any verb before it. This seems to decide for M. T. את was read by LXX as אות, as it was by Jerome and probably by the Hebrew reviser himself (cf. note on *v.* 12), and the sentence originally translated in the form in which the Lyons Heptateuch found it. Subsequently καὶ θήσεις was inserted.

תקוה, which was not before LXX, occurs only here and in *v.* 21. We no doubt owe it to the reviser who inserted 21 b;

perhaps the one who subsequently added the somewhat rare words הקף and מאסף in ch. vi. and חרש in *v.* 1 of this chapter.

19. τῷ ὅρκῳ σου τούτῳ. Probably an ampliative gloss. *vv.* 19 and 20 are wrongly divided in LXX.

20. אשר השבעתנו. Omit with LXX and substitute זאת as in *v.* 17.

21. ותקשר וגו'. Not in LXX. Hollenberg and others suggest that the eye of the scribe passed from the first ילכו to the second. But it must be urged that the action described is not suitable to the situation presupposed. It is not yet time for Rahab to display the cord. This was to be done "when we come into the city," *v.* 18. The spies are to be in hiding some days, and the Jordan crossed by the Israelites before the sign is required.

23. LXX omit ויבאו.

24. τὴν γῆν ἐκείνην. The last word is perhaps amplificatory.

CHAPTER III.

1. הוא וכל בני ישראל. Not in LXX. The usual phrase is "all Israel." Only elsewhere in Num. xxvii. 21 (C. and B.).

3. LXX. "The priests and the Levites" for "the priests the Levites." A common alteration in LXX.

4. במדה. LXX has στήσεσθε which should be emended to στήσασθε; they read the word as עמדו (imper.).

5. "Sanctify yourselves." LXX adds "for the morrow," perhaps rightly, cf. vii. 13.

8. ואתה. LXX = ועתה. It is difficult to see any reason for the pronoun being used here. There is no particular emphasis.

עד קצה. LXX B ἐπὶ μέσου. A and F ἐπὶ μέρους rightly, cf. the translation of קצה throughout this book, iii. 15, iv. 19 *et al.*

The LXX καὶ before ἐν τῷ Ἰορδανῃ is no doubt right, cf. Driver, *Tenses*, § 124, where the omission is noted. The waw fell out by haplography with the preceding nun.

10. LXX omit ויאמר יהושע. It occurs immediately before.

11. הברית is of course ungrammatical. This and the corresponding anomaly in *v.* 17 (הארון) are generally taken to show that the words following are insertions, if so they were in the text earlier than LXX. In the places where the ark is mentioned, *vv.* 3, 6, 8, 11, 13, 14, 15 *bis*, 17, LXX follows M.T.;

amplifying in *v.* 6 by Κυρίου and in *vv.* 13 and 15 by τῆς διαθήκης. (In *v.* 13 Κυρίου has to do duty for both אדון and יהוה, or *v.* 13 may have been originally the same as 11.) The facts here tabulated show that the translator of Joshua was, like other LXX translators, more inclined to add to, than to omit from the Hebrew text.

לפניכם. Not in LXX.

12. ועתה. Not in LXX. Inserted by a Hebrew scribe to give an air of connection to a verse which is plainly out of place.

13. כפות רגלי. LXX οἱ πόδες. The same phrase is rendered in the same way in iv. 18. Perhaps an abbreviation in both cases. But כף is literally rendered in i. 3.

Of the last six words, three are not represented in LXX. Following a hint of Dillmann we may conjecture that LXX represents an intermediate stage between the original Hebrew and the M. T. The verse originally ended at יכרתון. A scribe added the first three words of *v.* 16—to judge from the anomalous grammar of ויעמדו—quite mechanically. This text the LXX translator rendered. A later scribe, in order to make the two clauses correspond, introduced the remaining three words from *v.* 16.

15. τοῦ Ἰορδανου may be a dittograph. כל, LXX ὡσεί reading כ.

16. ἔστη πῆγμα ἕν. Many MSS. read εἰς πῆγμα ἕν.

באדם העיר אשר מצד צרתן. LXX σφοδρῶς ἕως μέρος Καριαθιαριμ = במאד עד אשר קצה כערתן. That is, באדם was read as במאד, עיר or rather ער was read as עד and עד אשר translated by ἕως. The ה of העיר in M. T. belongs to the name of the town. Μέρος for מצד is at first sight troublesome. It is translated rightly in xii. 9 by πλησίον. The translator uses μέρος to render קצה—which was written קץ—the outskirts of a city, and he no doubt read that here, mistaking מ for ק. The ד of מצד was taken with the following word and read as ך, and the צ of Zarethan read as ע. Hence Καριαθιμ (54 and 75) afterwards filled out to Kirjath Jearim. In spite of the mistakes made by LXX it enables us to restore the right reading עיר, not העיר, and consequently the true name of the city, Adamah. If the ה had been written, as it would had it been the article and not the termination of a word, the translator would not have taken ער for עד; the article would have kept him right.

17. הכן. Not in LXX BA, a late insertion from iv. 3.

CHAPTER IV.

In spite of the fact that we have only two narratives J and E (with Deut. amplifications) to deal with in this chapter, there are three accounts of the events connected with the memorial stones. They are (1) carried into the midst of the Jordan and set up there, *v.* 9, (2) carried out of the midst of the river from the place where the priests stood and set up on the land, 3 a, 5 and 8 a. But the command to carry the stones over העביר in 3 b and 8 b, points to a third account of the stones being taken right across from the East to the West side; so Wellhausen and Holzinger; Dillmann leaves it undecided. As to the existence of a third account the LXX renders some help. If with it we omit the phrase in *v.* 3 ממצב רגלי הכהנים we get two commands: (1) Take up from the midst of the Jordan, *v.* 3a, (2) Prepare or get ready (הכין[1]) twelve stones, and carry them across with you, and deposit them in the lodging place, where ye shall lodge this night, *v.* 3 b. The latter command is complete and natural, and may therefore be taken as part of the original narrative. The first command is incomplete and can fairly be put down to a scribe who was influenced by the account of the stones being taken out of the river. This account comes from *vv.* 5 and 8 a. In 8 a מתוך הירדן is not quite consistent with העביר in 8 b and can easily be dispensed with. Verse 5 however remains, but the LXX may indirectly help us here: עברו לפני יהוה אל תוך הירדן והרימו לכם איש אבן אחת על שכמו. The phrase אל תוך הירדן comes before הרימו, and if the men had been commanded to lift up the stones from the midst of the river, we should naturally expect משם after it, and indeed the LXX actually inserts ἐκεῖθεν, the equivalent of משם, but it is not in the M. T. This little point may put us on the right track. Was the sentence originally meant to convey no command at all to take up stones from the midst of the river? The fact that משם was not inserted after והרימו by the original writer is surely in favour of this. There is no doubt that as Carpenter and Battersby say "the narrative of the memorial stones is extraordinarily confused." It is here suggested that

[1] The same form would serve for both singular and plural.

this confusion was introduced by the misunderstanding of the writer's meaning in *v.* 5; a misunderstanding which arose from the position of הרימו after עברו. In the mind of the original writer there would be no suspicion of the possibility of his meaning being mistaken. Certain men are ordered to get ready—הכין—the stones; then Joshua gives the command "cross over before Jahveh, and take up the stones on your shoulders." The context made it clear that the stones to be shouldered were in readiness on the bank of the river, hence there could be no ambiguity caused by putting הרימו after עברו. As for מן הירדן in *v.* 20, it must be urged that מן is just as likely to represent מעבר as מתוך. With this interpretation of *v.* 5 we get rid of the strange statement that twelve stones were taken from the place where the priests' feet stood, get two accounts only of the stones in the two narratives, and are relieved of the hopeless grammatical difficulty of הכין in *v.* 3.

After the meaning of *v.* 5 had been misunderstood, 8a suffered interpolation by the words מתוך הירדן and 3 a by שאו מתוך הירדן. This was the state of the text before the LXX. Afterwards 3 a suffered a further interpolation by ממצב רגלי הכהנים from *v.* 9, and מזה from some later hand. Probably also *v.* 4 stated that Joshua called the men who had prepared the stones, but אשר הכינו האבנים was altered into אשר הכין מבני ישראל. Joshua does not 'prepare' the men, he 'takes' (לקח) them or 'commands' (צוה) or 'calls' (קרא) them; iii. 12, iv. 2, 3 a, 4.

2. קחו plural. LXX read the singular rightly, as Joshua alone is addressed.

3. לאמר. Not in LXX, probably not original; out of 43 occurrences in this book there are only four unrepresented, i. 13, iii. 6, iv. 3, iv. 22. See Intro., p. 6.

ממצב רגלי הכהנים. These words are omitted here in LXX, though they recur in *v.* 9 where they are in place and give perfectly good sense. To put twelve stones in the bed of the river where the priests stood, is quite a possible proceeding: but apart from the explanation of the origin of the phrase already given, it is difficult to believe that a first-hand narrator would have thought it possible that twelve—presumably large stones—could be taken from the limited area covered by the ark and its bearers. Holzinger however maintains deliberate omission on the part of LXX.

הכין. LXX ἑτοίμους reading נכונים, induced by the context. In the original text the two forms would only differ by one letter. Graetz, *Die Psalmen*, p. 132, gives examples of the confusion of ה and נ, and the context would strongly favour נ.

4. אשר הכין. LXX τῶν ἐνδόξων. The Hebrew shows this to be a corruption of οὓς ἐνέδειξεν. Examples of many equally bad corruptions can be seen in Driver's *Samuel*, p. lviii. See also in this book xv. 21, and xxiii. 4 where B has ὅπερ εἶπα for ἐπέρριφα.

5. 5 a has been amplified in the Hebrew by ארון and אלהיכם, see LXX. It is worth noticing that LXX has an interesting doublet here, ἔμπροσθέν μου and πρὸ προσώπου Κυρίου. The first expression shows that לפני יהוה was read as לפני; this could not have been done unless יהוה was abbreviated to י which did not differ in form from ו, לפני ו' became by haplography לפני. For other cases showing that יהוה was written as י or ו see Driver's *Samuel*, p. lxix, note 2; also ch. vi. 9 and xxiv. 7 of this book.

5 b. καὶ ἀνελόμενος ἐκεῖθεν ἕκαστος λίθον ἀράτω κ.τ.λ.

As pointed out above ἐκεῖθεν is an insertion. ἀράτω is not a free translation as Hollenberg suggests. It comes after λίθον in B corresponding exactly in position to אחת after אבן; it therefore represents the verb which was read by mistake instead of אחת, perhaps וּתְנוּ.

6. בקרבכם. LXX κείμενον διὰ παντός. The Hebrew must have been illegible, and the translator therefore supplied something suitable. κείμενος is very rarely used in the Greek Bible. This renders it probable that the word was the translator's own and not a rendering of any text before him. See on xiii. 14 b.

7. καὶ σύ. LXX read sing. for pl. as in vi. 3. Final ם was indicated by a mark of abbreviation. LXX is a little free here.

ארון ברית יהוה amplified in LXX by πάσης τῆς γῆς.

נכרתו מי הירדן. Not in LXX BA. It may have crept in from the preceding line.

8. למספר שבטי בני ישראל. LXX ἐν τῇ συντελείᾳ τῆς διαβάσεως τῶν υἱῶν.

In comparing these readings it must be noticed that בני ישראל and υἱῶν occupy the same position in the sentence; so that the problem is to see how למספר שבטי and ἐν τῇ συντελείᾳ τῆς διαβάσεως are connected.

It is true that at first sight one would take LXX to have

read בְּתֹם בני ישראל לעבר comparing iv. 1, 11. But the fact that בני ישראל and υἱῶν correspond in position forbids that; as the translation of iv. 1, 11 in LXX shows that the subject should come immediately after the verb.

בתם וגו' is therefore ruled out. But it seems impossible to find two Hebrew substantives to represent the two Greek substantives: we must therefore fall back on the suggestion that the Hebrew words before the translator were illegible and that he was obliged to supply the deficiency from his own sense of what was suitable, and on the basis of iv. 1 he wrote ἐν τῇ συντελείᾳ τῆς διαβάσεως. He probably read למספר as לעבר.

9. LXX ἄλλους inserted for harmonistic reasons; whether by the translator or a later hand it is impossible to say. αὐτῷ; in the Jordan itself, another addition.

10 b. "According to all," etc., LXX omits. Almost certainly an addition in M. T.

11. והכהנים לפני העם. LXX καὶ οἱ λίθοι ἔμπροσθεν αὐτῶν. αὐτῆς in 44, 54, 75, 76, 106 is no doubt right. Read therefore והאבנים לפניה. A natural circumstantial clause; the ark passed over "with the stones before it."

13. ערבת יריחו. LXX BA πρὸς τὴν Ἰεριχω πόλιν. According to five MSS. τὴν πόλιν Ἰεριχω.

The BA reading is earlier than the other, for that could arise from BA but not vice versa. But πόλιν itself is not original; πρὸς τὴν Ἰεριχω was the original phrase as can be seen from a comparison with ii. 1, iv. 19, vi. 2, 25, viii. 2, ix. 9 and x. 1, where the article alone is used. In all these cases we get τὴν Ἰεριχω τῇ or τῆς Ἰεριχω. LXX then either did not have ערבת in their text or else deliberately omitted it. But what motive could there be for omission? In the next chapter, v. 10, בערבת is translated by ἐπὶ δυσμῶν, and the same word would doubtless have been used here if the M. T. were right. The translator would have felt no hesitation in writing πρὸς δυσμὰς Ἰεριχω. The probability therefore is that ערבת was not in the text before LXX. In that case we get rid of a difficulty; for this verse has been assigned to P on the strength of the expression ערבת. But it has always been felt that the number of armed men, 40,000, here assigned to the 2½ tribes is in striking contrast to that given in Numb. xxvi. which belongs to P, where we get about 110,000. If however ערבת was not in the original, the necessity of assigning the verse to P vanishes; it will belong, like those which precede and follow, to a writer of the Deuteronomic school. In iii. 16 ערבה is transliterated, see also xi. 16.

14. γένους should represent עם, but עם ישראל does not occur in this book: viii. 33 must be corrected by LXX, see note; it is probably therefore an amplification.

18. נתקו. LXX καὶ ἔθηκαν not knowing the word. The right rendering in viii. 6 ἀποσπάω is a guess from the context as viii. 16 ἀφίστημι shows. LXX τοὺς πόδας for "the soles of the feet of the priests" is the result of this; the erroneous ἔθηκαν already had ἱερεῖς for its nom., and its repetition was unnecessary. On כפות רגלי see iii. 13.

21. LXX omits seven words in this verse. Hollenberg holds that the translator wished to render the diffuse Hebrew more concisely, but the fact that he renders the superfluous לכם in the similar passage in *v.* 6 is against this. ויאמר אל בני ישראל if original may have been omitted by homoioteleuton. מחר would be expected on the analogy of *v.* 6, but the 'fathers' who do not appear in *v.* 6 might easily be an insertion as elsewhere, cf. xxiv. 6 note.

22. The omission of לאמר in LXX after והודעתם is upheld by the same omission in M. T. *v.* 7 after ואמרתם, though strangely enough LXX inserts λέγων in *v.* 7.

24. למען יראתם. LXX ἵνα ὑμεῖς σέβησθε shows that the erroneous pointing is based on ancient tradition.

כל הימים. LXX ἐν παντὶ ἔργῳ. The MS must have been illegible.

CHAPTER V.

1. LXX BA omit כל, ימה, and כל of וכל; additions no doubt due to the hand of a reviser.

ימה, geographical detail not in LXX. καὶ ἐτάκησαν κ.τ.λ. is the doublet, κατεπλάγησαν the original.

2. שוב–שנית. LXX = שֵׁב. The reviser altered שב to שוב and added שנית at the end of the verse, see below on *v.* 8.

3. τοῦ καλουμένου, explanatory addition.

LXX *vv.* 4 b to 6 (slightly emended)	M. T. *vv.* 4 b to 6
All those who were born by the way and those who were uncircumcised of them that came out of Egypt, all these Joshua circumcised.	All the people who came out of Egypt, males, the men of war, died in the wilderness by the way when they had come out of Egypt.
	For circumcised were all the people who came out, but all the people who were born in the wilderness by the way when they had come out from Egypt were not circumcised.
For for forty years Israel wandered in the wilderness, therefore uncircumcised were most of them. As for the men of war who came out of the land of Egypt who disobeyed the commands of God, etc.	For for forty years the children of Israel walked in the wilderness until all the nation was consumed,—the men of war who came out of Egypt who did not hearken, etc.

4, 5, 6. Here we have a LXX text considerably different from that of M. T. The expression ὃν δὲ τρόπον cannot represent וזה הדבר אשר. The Greek should probably be taken as referring backwards, "So Joshua purified the children of Israel," while the Hebrew refers forward.

The probability is that LXX misread וזה as וכה and paraphrased מל by περιεκάθαρεν. Then 4 a in M. T. would stand. The text before LXX would be as follows: וזה הדבר אשר מל יהושע את בני ישראל: כל הילודים בדרך וכל הערלים מהיצאים ממצרים כל אלה מל יהושע

6. In LXX this verse gives a very different meaning from that which is expected. It is unanimously admitted to be wrong. I venture to propose the following solution. αὐτῶν τῶν μαχίμων = in Hellenistic Greek "those fighting men," see Blass, p. 170, but it is doubtful whether the translator had before him אנשי המלחמה ההם. He probably translated somewhat mechanically the following text[1], after the words "The

[1] Taking מהם to be in apposition to אנשי המלחמה and thus translating by αὐτῶν τῶν μαχίμων. Yet it is possible that LXX originally translated correctly by οἱ μάχιμοι κ.τ.λ., for 75 in Holmes and Parsons gives οἱ ἐξελθωτες which may be the remains of the original unassimilated οἱ ἐξεληλυθότες.

children of Israel wandered forty years in the wilderness" לכן ערלים היו רבים מהם אנשי המלחמה היצאים ממצרים אשר לא שמעו בקול יהוה אשר נשבע להם לבלתי הראותם את הארץ. This it is true gives neither grammar nor sense. But if we put a stop at מהם and omit the אשר before נשבע, which may easily have crept in under the influence of the preceding אשר, we get both sense and grammar, and can then render:

> "For the children of Israel had wandered forty years in the wilderness, therefore uncircumcised were most of them. As for the men of war who came out of Egypt, who did not obey the voice of Jehovah, he had sworn to them that he would not let them see the land," etc.

The LXX translator had no reason for altering his text, the Hebrew reviser had: viz. the strong objection he would feel to the statement that some of those who came up out of Egypt were uncircumcised. This could not be admitted: but it was asserted in the original text and therefore considerable alteration was necessary to bring the passage into harmony with the religious beliefs of the reviser. Dillmann (p. 458) speaks of "this not very clear exposition," but considering the difficulty of the task, the overworking has on the whole been ingeniously done.

δύο in LXX is simply a corrupt repetition and misreading of שנה.

7 b. כי ערלים היו כי לא מלו אתם בדרך. LXX B *διὰ τὸ αὐτοὺς γεγεννῆσθαι κατὰ τὴν ὁδὸν ἀπεριτμήτους* = כי הילודים בדרך היו ערלים. The Hebrew may possibly have been כי ערלים היו כי יִלְּדוּ בדרך, but הילודים which appears in M. T. in this passage is perhaps more likely. When the translator began with *διά* for כי he was obliged to go on with the acc. and inf.

8. כל הגוי. Not in LXX BA. Thus LXX is consistent here. In view of Numb. xiv. כל הגוי had to be supported by שנית and שוב in *v.* 2. According to the narrative in Numbers exclusion from the promised land was pronounced on those Israelites who were 20 years old and upwards. This took place two years after the Exodus: therefore all those who were under 18 years of age at that time had been born in Egypt, and according to M. T. here, must have been circumcised. But here all the nation —כל הגוי—is said to have been circumcised at Gilgal. Thus those male Israelites who at the time of the sentence of exclusion

were under 18 years of age and survived to the time of entry, must have been circumcised twice. Hence שנית and שוב in *v.* 2.

Here as elsewhere LXX appears to give an intermediate stage in the history of the text. As Dillmann (p. 459) says, the section 4—7 is an endeavour to bring the account of the circumcision at Gilgal into harmony with Genesis xvii.

In LXX we have the record of an attempt that was not drastic enough for subsequent editors: in M.T. we have the final endeavour of one or more scribes to achieve the impossible.

9. עד היום הזה. Not in LXX. Carpenter and Battersby point out that here and in vii. 26 occur the only two instances of the omission of these words from LXX Josh.

10. ויחנו and בגלגל not represented in LXX. They may have been omitted by homoioteleuton. If so the LXX supplied an explicit subject to ויעשו. Carpenter and Battersby, however, point out that v. 10 (P) is the continuation of iv. 19 (P) and in the original narrative the words omitted in *v.* 10 would not be required. The impression conveyed by inspection of the Hebrew text no doubt is that the last three words of *v.* 9 and the first four of *v.* 10 were omitted by accident, but the insertion of geographical details in other places renders the same thing possible here.

בערבות יריחו. Represented in LXX by a doublet or rather a triplet: (1) ἐπὶ δυσμῶν Ἰεριχω—see same mistake in Psalm lxviii. 4 and often—xi. 16; (2) τῷ πέραν τοῦ Ἰορδανου; (3) ἐν τῷ πεδίῳ. In (2) ערבת was read as עבר, and τοῦ Ἰορδανου added.

11. ממחרת הפסח omitted in LXX BA. As in *v.* 12 ממחרת is also omitted, it seems likely that these words were not in the text of the translator. See Intro., p. 3.

קלוי. LXX νέα, a mistake.

12. ויאכלו מתבואת ארץ כנען. LXX B ἐκαρπίσαντο δὲ τὴν κουρὰν τῶν φ. All other MSS. seem to have χωράν = ארץ.

תבואה occurs only here in Joshua and the translator may possibly have been in doubt as to its meaning and omitted it: but καρπίζομαι means "to enjoy the fruit of," so ἐκαρπίσαντο is most probably an idiomatic translation.

In 14 and 15 וישתחו and ויעש יהושע כן are not in LXX BA. For the latter cf. x. 23. Probably editorial.

CHAPTER VI.

There are striking differences between M. T. and LXX in this chapter. Verses 3 b and 4 in M. T. are not represented in LXX. Verses 8 and 9 are narrative in M. T. and a command in LXX. The rearguard with trumpets which appears in *vv.* 9 and 13 of M. T. is not represented in LXX.

The explanation which has generally been offered of these differences is that LXX shortened M. T. to avoid difficulties. See Introduction, p. 11, in opposition to this.

1. מפני בני ישראל. Not in LXX. Verse 1 is a participial introductory clause (Ewald, 341 c) = "now when Jericho had shut its gates and was shut up, none going out and none coming in, then Jehovah said unto Joshua." The omission of the three words lightens the clause.

2. גבורי החיל. The absence of any connecting particle shows that the text has suffered somehow, but LXX with τοὺς δυνατοὺς ἐν ἰσχύι renders no help. Before these words however LXX has τὸν βασιλέα αὐτῆς τὸν ἐν αὐτῇ = ואת מלכה אשר בה. Perhaps we should read אשר בה (or comparing ix. 10 which shows that יושב could easily fall out after אשר, אשר יושב בה) with the singular. Or if the plural is to be retained, we might emend אשר בה into וישביה or ואנשיה, "I will deliver into thy hand Jericho and its king and its inhabitants, the mighty men of valour." For the omission of את before the second object, cf. Davidson, *Heb. Syn.*, § 72, R 2. Cf. x. 2 of Gibeon וכל אנשיה גבורים.

3. וסבתם. LXX = וסבת.

3 b and 4. Not in LXX. Insertion of reviser, see Introduction, p. 11.

5. בשמעכם את קול השופר. Not in LXX. The absence of a connecting particle raises the suspicion that the phrase is a mere variation of the preceding words, inserted when it was seen that in *vv.* 16 and 20 the signal was given by blowing the שופרות.

נגדו. LXX κατὰ πρόσωπον εἰς τὴν πόλιν. At first sight the question seems to be whether העירה was in the M. T. as in *v.* 20, or whether εἰς τὴν πόλιν is an addition of the LXX scribe. But the truth is that εἰς τὴν πόλιν is original and κατὰ πρόσωπον a doublet. The translator knew the exact meaning of נגד, see

iii. 16 *ἀπέναντι*, v. 13 *ἐναντίον*, viii. 11 *ἐξ ἐναντίας*. The free rendering of נגד in viii. 35 by *εἰς τὰ ὦτα* suggests that *εἰς τὴν πόλιν* is his rendering of the word here, and *κατὰ πρόσωπον* which he never uses for נגד, a later doublet. An interesting example of the truth of Lagarde's second canon.

6. שאו וגו״. Omit with LXX as insertion of reviser: the last nine words of the verse from ושבעה onwards are repeated from the interpolation in *v.* 4. Both are anticipatory insertions from *vv.* 8 and 13.

7. Omission in LXX of ארון before Jahveh as in vii. 6. *περιελθεῖν* must be emended to *παρελθεῖν* as it represents עברו.

8. הכהנים. LXX has no article. After the insertion of 3b, 4 the article was required in M. T. LXX imperatives are original.

9. In LXX this verse is quite intelligible though in re-translation it requires the insertion of a word after *ἔμπροσθεν*. *οἱ δὲ μάχιμοι ἔμπροσθεν παραπορευέσθωσαν, καὶ οἱ ἱερεῖς οἱ οὐραγοῦντες ὀπίσω τῆς κιβωτοῦ τῆς διαθήκης Κυρίου σαλπίζοντες.*

The first difficulty is with *ἔμπροσθεν*. What does it represent? לפנים which the translator probably thought he had before him is impossible: it is used with the meaning 'before' of time only, not of position. In accordance with usage some object is desiderated. Comparison with *v.* 13, where the instructions here given are carried out, would be the best means of deciding, but is precluded by the fact that the verse is corrupt. We must therefore resort to 13 M. T., and there we find not an exact repetition of M. T. 9 but a shorter expression לפניהם. This may be accepted as having been the original in *v.* 9, though it may be pointed out that there is something to be said for לפני י׳. Supposing this to have been written, there would be in the text three exactly similar letters together: the last letter of לפני, the י representing יהוה and the ו of והמאסף. One of these might easily have disappeared or have been overlooked by the translator. In default however of *v.* 13 LXX we must perhaps be content to follow M. T. 13, and accept לפניהם as being before LXX in *v.* 9. The Hebrew reviser either expanded "before them" or altered "before J." into "before the priests blowing with the trumpets."

The second difficulty is with καὶ οἱ ἱερεῖς οἱ οὐραγοῦντες. Lucian and many MSS omit οἱ οὐραγοῦντες. According to Field, Cod. VII, second corrector has οἱ ἀκολουθοῦντες. Syro-Hex. has "and those who went after," evidently reading the same. Lyons Hept. has, et sacerdotes qui sequuntur post arcam testamenti tubis canant. On this evidence we may conjecture that LXX read something like והכהנים ההלכים אחרי ארון יהוה יתקעו, and that המאסף is a correction. As for παραπορευέσθωσαν, Wellhausen's statement (*Die Comp.*[3] p. 122) that *vv.* 8 and 9 were originally commands upholds the LXX imperatives in these verses.

11. את העיר הקף. Omitted by B; הקף is almost certainly due to the hand of a reviser.

פעם אחת. LXX εὐθέως. The translator does not appear to have known the meaning of פעם. In *v.* 14 he gives ἐγγύθεν, 16 περίοδος; the right rendering in *v.* 15 must be a guess. In x. 42 he gives εἰσάπαξ.

12. LXX inserts here καὶ τῇ ἡμέρᾳ τῇ δευτέρᾳ and omits ביום השני in *v.* 14. Comparison with *v.* 15 favours LXX.

13 b and 14[1]. The following conspectus is from Holzinger:

B.	A.	Lucian.
(1) καὶ μετὰ ταῦτα εἰσεπορεύοντο οἱ μάχιμοι καὶ ὁ λοιπὸς ὄχλος ὄπισθε τῆς κιβωτοῦ τῆς διαθήκης κυρίου.	(2) καὶ οἱ ἱερεῖς ἐσάλπισαν ταῖς σάλπιγξιν	(1) καὶ ὁ λοιπὸς ὄχλος ἅπας καὶ οἱ μάχιμοι εἰσεπορεύοντο μετὰ ταῦτα καὶ ὁ λοιπὸς ὄχλος ὄπισθεν τῆς κιβωτοῦ τῆς διαθήκης κυρίου.
(2) καὶ οἱ ἱερεῖς ἐσάλπισαν ταῖς σάλπιγξι.	(3) καὶ ὁ λοιπὸς ὄχλος ἅπας. καὶ ἀπῆλθον πάλιν εἰς τὴν παρεμβολήν.	(2) πορευόμενοι καὶ σαλπίζοντες ταῖς κερατίναις.
(3) καὶ ὁ λοιπὸς ὄχλος ἅπας περιεκύκλωσε τὴν πόλιν ἐγγύθεν καὶ ἀπῆλθον πάλιν εἰς τὴν παρεμβολήν.	(1) καὶ μετὰ ταῦτα εἰσεπορεύοντο οἱ μάχιμοι καὶ ἱ λοιπὸς ὄχλος ὄπισθεν τῆς κιβωτοῦ τῆς διαθήκης κυρίου.	(3) καὶ περιεκύκλωσαν τὴν πόλιν ἐν τῇ ἡμέρᾳ τῇ δευτέρᾳ ἅπαξ ἐγγύθεν καὶ ἀπῆλθον πάλιν εἰς τὴν παρεμβολήν.
37 words.	33 words.	43 words.

[1] *v.* 14 in Swete should begin at καὶ ὁ λοιπὸς ὄχλος ἅπας.

The LXX here is very corrupt: is it possible to restore the true text? I venture to think it is. For taking *v.* 14b first and comparing it with M. T. we should naturally infer that LXX inserted ὁ λοιπὸς ὄχλος ἅπας as an explicit subject of ויסבו. If this is so, it gives us the origin of ὁ λοιπὸς ὄχλος in *v.* 13[1]; which offers a simple solution of an otherwise hopeless problem. For striking out ὁ λοιπὸς ὄχλος in *v.* 13 we get in B: καὶ μετὰ ταῦτα εἰσεπορεύοντο οἱ μάχιμοι ὄπισθε τῆς κιβωτοῦ τῆς διαθήκης κυρίου καὶ οἱ ἱερεῖς ἐσάλπισαν ταῖς σάλπιγξι.

That μετὰ ταῦτα is an intrusion is seen from its place being different in BA, and Lucian. Omitting it and turning the rest back into Hebrew, we get

והחלוץ הלך אחרי ארון ברית יהוה והכהנים תקעי השופרות :

This leaves us the statement "The armed men going *behind* the ark of the covenant of Jehovah and the priests blowing the horns": now compare the two texts.

LXX = והחלוץ הלך אחרי ארון ברית יהוה.

M. T. והחלוץ הלך לפניהם והמאסף הלך אחרי ארון יהוה. This shows how the mistake arose. The translator's eye passed from the first הלך to the second, the result being the statement that the armed men followed the ark. This was felt by subsequent Greek scribes to be wrong, and various endeavours were made to improve matters by the introduction of ὁ λοιπὸς ὄχλος from below and the insertion of οἱ ἱερεῖς to get a subject to ἐσάλπισαν. Indications of these endeavours are to be seen in the confused condition of the passage in all three Recensions, copied above.

The above solution is confirmed by an inspection of Lucian's text—οἱ μάχιμοι εἰσεπορεύοντο μετὰ ταῦτα καὶ ὁ λοιπὸς ὄχλος ὄπισθεν τῆς κιβωτοῦ. Striking out ὁ λοιπὸς ὄχλος, we get μετὰ ταῦτα and ὄπισθεν together. Omitting μετὰ ταῦτα, we are left with οἱ μάχιμοι εἰσεπορεύοντο ὄπισθεν τῆς κιβωτοῦ. This turned back into Hebrew and compared with M. T. gives us the same result as before, viz. that the present LXX text arose from omission by homoioteleuton and subsequent endeavours to avoid a glaring contradiction.

We may now restore the Greek text as it left the hand of the translator, approximately as follows:

[1] ὁ λοιπὸς ὄχλος in 13 incurs suspicion from the fact that if the translator had once got the excellent rendering οὐραγέω for מאסף he would not be likely to desert it for the vague ὁ λοιπὸς ὄχλος.

13 b. καὶ εἰσεπορεύοντο οἱ μάχιμοι (omission of לפניהם והמאסף הלך[1]) ὄπισθεν τῆς κιβωτοῦ τῆς διαθήκης κυρίου. καὶ ἐσάλπισαν ταῖς σάλπιγξι. 14. καὶ ὁ λοιπὸς ὄχλος ἅπας περιεκύκλωσε τὴν πόλιν.

ὁ λοιπὸς ὄχλος ἅπας is an explicit subject. When it was seen that the text stated that the armed men went behind the ark, καὶ ὁ λοιπὸς ὄχλος was inserted before ὄπισθεν, but ὁ λοιπὸς ὄχλος could not be allowed to blow the trumpets, accordingly οἱ ἱερεῖς was inserted before ἐσάλπισαν.

15. LXX B ἑξάκις. Perhaps rightly. Six was altered to seven when the next clause was inserted.

רק ביום וגו'. Might have been omitted in LXX by homoioteleuton, but Dillmann takes it as belonging to R so that it was probably not in the text. If a clause is an addition to the original text and is not represented in LXX, the natural conclusion is that it was later than LXX.

כמשפט הזה. Not in LXX in this verse, while in *v.* 8 ὡσαύτως has no equivalent in the Hebrew. Both may be insertions in the respective texts.

17. LXX omit the last seven words. The word מלאכים for the spies is against their genuineness. The spies were not מלאכים at all.

18. Read with LXX השמרו; reflexive Niphal.

תחרימו. LXX ἐνθυμηθέντες = תחמדו, so Hollenberg followed by all moderns.

19. וכלי. Omitted by LXX here and in *v.* 24.

20. וירע העם. Omitted by LXX. It has probably crept in from the next line ויריעו העם. καὶ ἰσχυρῷ is ampliative.

נגדו. If, as appears likely, נגדו is rendered by εἰς τὴν πόλιν, העירה is an insertion in M. T.; see on *v.* 5.

"And they took the city." Not in LXX. Probably an insertion by the scribe who omitted אותה in the next verse.

21. ושה. Not in LXX. It destroys the symmetry of the verse.

22. כאשר נשבעתם לה. Not in LXX. May have been omitted by homoioteleuton; but cf. ii. 17 and 20. On other differences in 22 and 23 see next note.

23. Transpose את כל אשר לה and the next three words as in LXX.

[1] These words are left as they stand in M. T., though as 9 and 13 would, mutatis mutandis, be the same, the last two are probably due to the alteration of the reviser; and we should no doubt read והכהנים ההלכים.

In *v.* 22 after מרגלים, M. T. has הארץ, which is not represented in LXX. In *v.* 23 M. T. has no object after מרגלים, while LXX has τὴν πόλιν. As in Gen. xlii. מרגלים is used six times absolutely and also in Josh. ii. 1, 1 Sam. xxvi. 4 and 2 Sam. xv. 10; we may conclude that the word had come to be a substantive pure and simple and that הארץ in *v.* 22 M. T. is an insertion and also τὴν πόλιν in *v.* 23 LXX. After τὴν πόλιν the LXX further inserted εἰς οἰκίαν τῆς γυναικός. In 22 M. T. has הזונה and in 23 LXX after Rahab has τὴν πόρνην. Perhaps also here both words are insertions.

24. בית. Omit with LXX. Cf. a similar insertion in ix. 23.

25. את כל אשר לה. Not in LXX. May have been an insertion from *v.* 22 or may have been omitted on account of its recent occurrence.

מלאכים. LXX had מרגלים. M. T. was altered in accordance with the insertion in *v.* 17.

26. לפני יהוה. The different position of ἐναντίον κυρίου in LXX B and in M. T., and its omission in A, show it to be no part of the original text.

את יריחו. Not in LXX. Superfluous after the words "this city."

LXX = 1 Kings xvi. 34. Hollenberg argues that the different wording of the LXX verse here from that in Kings precludes dependence. Another argument is found in the translation of the name of the younger son, perhaps some derivative of ישע, by διασωθέντι, as though it were a common part of speech and not a proper name. Further it is to be noted that the verse is absent from Kings in Lucian. This also favours the view that the passage here is the original.

Wellhausen's analysis of *vv.* 3—20 can be used to support LXX. He has disentangled the simplest form of the older narrative in M. T., and this can be shown to be an elaboration of a still older tradition which was preserved in LXX untouched in *vv.* 3—5, while in M. T. it has been edited out of all recognition. Verses 3—5 LXX contain the oldest tradition on which the rest of Wellhausen's narrative No. 1 is based. The fact that we expect between *vv.* 3 and 4 LXX some such words as 'seven days' or 'seven times' is due entirely to our impressions drawn from the rest of the chapter. It is owing to the Massoretic insertion in *v.* 3 that we translate "Ye shall go round the city." The words without the insertion would naturally mean 'surround the city.' This is LXX translation; which shows that they had no part of M. T. insertion before them. They gave the word its natural meaning—see Ox. *Lexicon*, סבב, 2 *a*, which shows that the meaning 'march round' hardly occurs outside this passage. The earliest narrative from which J. drew and which he elaborated contained nothing whatever about marching round the city. Surround the city, was the command, and when ye hear the sound of the trumpet, shout; and the walls shall fall down and all the people shall go up straight before them. This earliest tradition was probably enlarged as the result of a misunderstanding of the verb סבב which was probably induced by a desire to bring in the ark and give it the same position it had in the narrative of crossing the Jordan. When the word was once taken to mean 'march round the city,' the tradition could easily be enlarged to the narrative of J. as given by Wellhausen, minus *vv.* 3 and 4.

For a similar erroneous expansion based on a misunderstood expression, cf. the story of Jael and Sisera in Judges: see Robertson Smith, *O. T. J. C.*[2] p. 132. Further, most scholars recognise that J. drew from earlier narratives, the result being inconsistencies in J. itself: see Wellhausen, *Die Comp.*[3] p. 7 ff.

Both these processes have been united here. In one and the same narrative we have a piece drawn from an older source to which has been joined an elaboration largely based on the misunderstanding of a word in that older source: a probable story thus being made into an improbable one. That an army should surround a city and take it by assault is a probable story; that an army should march round a city once a day for seven days before assaulting it, is highly improbable. The further enlargement by later writers needs no comment.

CHAPTER VII.

1. *ἐνοσφίσαντο*. Inserted to give the full meaning. *μεγάλην* is ampliative.

עכן. LXX Ἀχαρ. Perhaps rightly as it is upheld by the paronomasia in *v.* 25.

2. LXX omits some of the geographical details as elsewhere, see Intro., p. 5. In addition, ויאמר אליהם is probably an insertion. If we compare this verse with ii. 1, where similar phraseology is

used, we find וישלח followed by לאמר without the intervention of ויאמר. This supports the LXX here in its omission of the expression.

3. תינע. LXX ἀναγάγῃς; a guess.

4. מן העם שמה. Not in LXX.

5. עד שברים. Geographical detail not in LXX.

6. ארון. Not in LXX. See on vi. 7.

7 and 8. אהה אדני. LXX δέομαι κύριε = בי אדני. The proper place of בי אדני is at the beginning of the request. Hence LXX is probably right in reading בי אדני here and omitting it at the beginning of *v.* 8. At the beginning of *v.* 8 M. T. has בי אדני מה, LXX καὶ τί ἐρῶ = ומה אמר, both more in accordance with probability.

7. הואלנו. LXX κατεμείναμεν. LXX did not know the word.

9. וישמעו. LXX καὶ ἀκούσας points to ושמעו. The first waw is a repetition of the last waw of איביו, waw and yod were indistinguishable. By accident וושמעו was written and the second ו taken for yod.

11. κλέψαντες is perhaps a free translation of לקחו and גנבו. כחשו is probably an addition to M. T. The word is rightly translated in xxiv. 27.

14. ונקרבתם. LXX καὶ συναχθήσεσθε = ונקבצתם. As קרב is the word used throughout the passage, LXX may have misread the word.

15. בחרם. Not in LXX. Plainly a gloss. Omit אתו with LXX.

17. κατὰ δήμους LXX = מִשְׁפְּחֹת. In this respect obviously superior to M. T.

וַיִּלְכֹּד את. All the versions read וַיִּלָּכֵד or ותלכד. The את crept in under the influence of the preceding את which is in place.

17 b. LXX omits the words after the first occurrence of לגברים up to and including the second. The fact that M. T. has לגברים twice, upholds Hollenberg's contention that the LXX shorter text is original, and that M. T. has been expanded by a scribe who wished 16 and 17 to conform to 14 in mentioning tribes, clans, households and individuals. It is worth noticing that the LXX here is upheld by the full text of 1 Sam. x. 21, where the משפחה, not the בית, is taken man by man. See Driver, *in loco.* LXX however by vocalising ויקרב wrongly may have omitted the second occurrence of יהודה and of זרחי.

19. בני. Omitted in LXX. LXX has σήμερον later on, which may be a misreading of בני.

21. אדרת. A cloak. A rare word. LXX ψιλήν, a carpet.

טובה. LXX B omits. Probably a gloss to explain the word שנער, the meaning of which was not well known, as is shown by LXX ποικίλην.

משקלו. Not in LXX.

23. כל בני ישראל. LXX = זקני, which is much more appropriate. Joshua and the Elders who are mentioned in *v.* 6 would naturally form the court of judgement.

ויצקם. LXX ἔθηκαν = ויצגם; cf. 2 Samuel xv. 24 for a similar case.

24. It is generally agreed that this verse has been considerably revised in the Hebrew, but whether before or after the original Greek translation is disputed.

The attainment of the original text in the Hebrew is lightened by the fact that M. T. (followed by LXX as we have it) betrays the hand of the reviser in the anomalous position of the words "and all Israel (LXX the people) with him" which are separated from the other words to which they naturally belong by a considerable interval. We can take the intervening words as an insertion based on the phrase "all that he hath" in *v.* 15. The LXX however as we have it (with a difference to be noted below) corresponds to the interpolated M. T. Was this interpolated M. T. before the original translator? Hollenberg denies this and points out that the suspected words are not rendered in the translator's usual style. Here we have the rigorous rendering of the suffixes, a method of procedure unlike that of the translator of whom Hollenberg rightly says (p. 6) "Er übersetzt die Suffixe oft nicht."

This is rendered still more probable by the fact that we have in A (*v.* 24 last clause) αὐτόν, and in B 25 αὐτόν. Had the interpolated words been in the text before LXX, αὐτόν would have been almost impossible. (The insertion of a late interpolation here and the omission of one in c. xx. tends to show that no *systematic* revision of LXX was undertaken.)

M. T. also has at the beginning of *v.* 24 "the silver, the cloak, and the wedge of gold." These words are not in B, A or F, and are therefore the insertion of a second Hebrew reviser.

καὶ ἀνήγαγεν αὐτὸν εἰς φάραγγα Ἀχώρ is a doublet due to a LXX reviser.

25. LXX inserts after "and Joshua said," τῷ Ἀχαρ. It makes prominent the grim paronomasia.

As pointed out in the Introduction, p. 13, LXX *v.* 26 speaks of punishment only by stoning: whereas *v.* 15 threatens punishment by burning: while M. T. reads They stoned him—they burnt them—they stoned them. If LXX represents the original text we must conclude that it was inconsistent; it threatened burning and recorded stoning and the translator followed his text faithfully.

26. עד היום הזה (1°). Not in LXX. Editorial addition; cf. v. 9.

It is possible that the original story narrated the death of Achan only; in support of this we may refer to xxii. 20.

CHAPTER VIII.

1. ואת עמו ואת עירו. Omitted in LXX BA. Probably an editorial addition to M. T.

2. ולמלכה (1°) may have been omitted accidentally from LXX BA. The second ולמלכה would seem to confirm the first.

4. ראו. Omitted by LXX as also מאד at the end of the clause.

לעיר (1°). LXX omit. It is certainly not wanted. ארב is construed with ל in *v.* 2 and *v.* 14, perhaps therefore the Hebrew reviser is responsible for the insertion from a desire for uniformity of construction.

6. נסים. The participle without a subject is anomalous. LXX Φεύγουσιν οὗτοι, which shows that they read נסים המה. The participle is emphatic and therefore precedes in accordance with Driver's *Tenses* 135. 4.

ונסנו לפניהם. Omit with LXX BA. Repeated from end of *v.* 5 where it is in place.

7. הורשתם. LXX πορεύσεσθε. Holzinger points out that in *v.* 11 πορεύεσθαι is used to translate נגש. Therefore emend to נגשתם אל.

7 b and 8 a. The omission of these words in LXX may be accidental. The setting on fire of the city would probably be

commanded. But it might be a harmonising or 'anticipatory' insertion from *v.* 19.

8. כדבר יהוה. Read with LXX כדבר הזה. For a similar confusion of יהוה and הזה see 1 Sam. ii. 23, where LXX gives *παντὸς τοῦ λαοῦ κυρίου* which probably represents כל העם הזה. See Driver, *in loco.*

9. וילן to end of verse omitted by LXX. Holzinger thinks the omission deliberate, to make the narrative less difficult, but

(1) No difficulty could be felt at the statement just before וישכם. (2) The fact that the same words (for וילן and וילך were originally the same, see Ezra x. 6) are omitted in *v.* 13 raises the suspicion that we have here a case of 'double insertion.'

11 b, 12, 13 a. From ויחנו מצפון to מצפון לעיר.

These verses are not in LXX and their omission removes a great stumbling block, viz. the second account of the ambush against Ai, with its striking discrepancy with regard to the number of men.

The first and perhaps natural inference is that the omission was intentional. It is felt to be (1) too long and (2) too convenient to be accidental.

But it is difficult to believe that the translator of chapter vi. 6—8 and of vii. 15 and 25 should have been so sensitive to contradictions as to remember that *v.* 3 of this chapter was inconsistent with *v.* 12 with respect to the number of men in the ambush. And indeed had that been the case, there would have been open to him the simple expedient of making the numbers correspond. But is accidental omission impossible? The fact that the omission begins after the words נגד העיר and ends with לעיר makes it possible that we have here another case of homoioteleuton. If the omission is felt to be suspiciously long—29 words—it may be pointed out that in the Hebrew text of 1 Sam. xiv. 41 twenty-three words are omitted[1]; and moreover the text before LXX may easily have been shorter than ours. See also Introduction, p. 13. Perhaps however a better solution is that of Steuernagel, who suggests that a later editor incorporated a second account found in some other MSS.

13 b. וילך וגו׳. Omit with LXX. The corresponding words

[1] Over *forty* words are omitted in 2 Samuel xi. 22. In Joshua xxi. *vv.* 36 and 37 are omitted from many MSS of the Hebrew Text by homoioteleuton.

in *v.* 9 are also omitted. This double omission tells in favour of LXX. Moreover if these words had been present here in the Hebrew exemplar, we should have to suppose that the translator (1) omitted a large number of words from ויחנו to מצפון לעיר, (2) picked out the words עקבו מים לעיר = καὶ τὰ ἔνεδρα τῆς πόλεως ἀπὸ θαλάσσης, and (3) then omitted the rest of the sentence.

14. LXX gives the better text, as is shown by M. T. itself in the phrase הוא וכל עמו which condemns אנשי העיר; the explicit subject was introduced when the preceding verbs were wrongly read as plural.

למועד לפני הערבה. Not in LXX. The words are very difficult: Kittel in his history says "the place is the same as J's מדבר." It may however be the insertion of the reviser who perhaps also altered the next verse with the same end in view, viz. to make it plain that the retreat was premeditated. The מועד would then indicate the place which the reviser assumed Joshua would take up, in order to draw away the enemy as far as possible from the town. Bennett, Holzinger, and Driver emend to למורד.

ישראל. LXX ἐπ' εὐθείας. The Hebrew word was misread as ישר. Ehrlich's suggestion of אל מישור is negatived by the fact that מישור in this book is always transliterated.

15. וינגעו. נגע is never used of smiting in battle. Ox. *Lex.* and others suggest ינגפו. LXX gives καὶ ἴδεν καὶ ἀνεχώρησεν κ.τ.λ. = וירא וינס יהושע וכל ישראל לפניהם. If this is original one can only suggest that the Hebrew reviser wished to bring out the point that the retreat was a feint and substituted the Niphal tolerativum "to allow oneself to be beaten."

15 b and 16 a. Not in LXX. It may have been omitted by homoioteleuton: note לפניהם–אחריהם. On the other hand there are good reasons for considering it to be no part of the text before LXX. For besides the want of a satisfactory reason for the omission here, 20 b, the other passage where המדבר occurs, is also absent from LXX, and there is an additional reason besides that absence for regarding it as an insertion (see note). Both passages may have their origin in *v.* 24 and will therefore have some affinity with what may be called 'anticipatory insertions' referred to on p. 6, line 29.

ויזעקו כל העם. Amplificatory of הוא וכל עמו in 14. The reviser was not content with this but in 17 a inserts ובית אל. All the people of Ai and of Bethel also, joined in the pursuit!

16 b. יהושע. LXX בני ישראל, which is justified by M. T. *v.* 17 last word (so Steuernagel).

18. אל העי. LXX ἐπὶ τὴν πόλιν = אל העיר. In the next clause M. T. has אל העיר.

In *v.* 18 LXX we read "Stretch out thy hand with the spear which is in thy hand." This arouses no suspicion, but it should be noticed that M. T. omits the first mention of the hand. Later in the verse LXX has "and Joshua stretched out his hand, the spear"; τὸν γαῖσον (M. T. "the spear which he had in his hand"), where the variations in the readings (see Field) show that τὸν γαῖσον is plainly an insertion. Again, in *v.* 19 it is stated simply that "Joshua stretched out his hand," no mention being made of the javelin; and finally *v.* 26 which states that "Joshua drew not his hand back wherewith he had stretched out the spear" is entirely omitted in LXX. We thus have in this section the omission of יד in M. T. in 18 a, the insertion of τὸν γαῖσον in 18 b LXX, the mention of the hand only in *v.* 19, and the omission in LXX of *v.* 26. These facts all tend to show that the reference to the javelin has certainly been amplified by the Hebrew reviser, while it is quite possible that the original narrative contained nothing about a javelin at all. It was perhaps inserted in order to make explicit what was no doubt a fact, that the leader would have some kind of weapon in his hand. Lyons Hept., with a shorter LXX text than any we now have, gives in *v.* 18 Extende manum tuam in Gaet civitatem, and in the next clause "in Gaet super civitatem." "In Gaet" represents ἐν γαίσῳ not ἐν Γαι. Hollenberg's suggestion that the translator omitted the word because he did not know its meaning will not hold in face of the numerous guesses in the book.

καὶ τὰ ἔνεδρα κ.τ.λ. = והאורב יקום מהרה ממקומו. This may be an insertion of LXX to show why the hand was stretched out, unless the Hebrew reviser omitted it in order to get room for his own insertion.

20. ולא היה בהם ידים. LXX οὐκ ἔτι εἶχον = להם. Ehrlich suggests that LXX rightly understood ידים in the sense of space, hence ποῦ.

20 b. Omit with LXX; the "turning back" does not come to pass till after 21 a and is there mentioned in the right place.

21. After העיר (2°) LXX has εἰς τὸν οὐρανόν; it may be an insertion from *v.* 20.

22. ויהיו לישראל בתוך is an awkward phrase. LXX gives ἀναμέσον τῆς παρεμβολῆς = בתוך המחנה. In all probability the text should be simply ויהיו בתוך, τῆς παρεμβολῆς being explanatory.

24. המדבר. As noticed above LXX does not render המדבר. It has ἐν τῷ ὄρει ἐπὶ τῆς καταβάσεως, which Dillmann, followed by Holzinger, translates by בהר במורד. בהר is of course a gloss on במורד. It is quite possible that במדבר is a corruption of an unglossed text: the waw of מורד belongs to the root and would be written. This would give the origin of מדבר in *vv.* 15 and 20.

ויפלו כלם לפי חרב. Omitted in LXX. An awkwardly attached amplification.

25. אנשי העי. LXX = ישבי, to be preferred in view of the statement that both men and women were slain.

26. It is generally suggested that this verse has been omitted in LXX by homoioteleuton, but it interrupts the narrative and may well be a gloss on the basis of Ex. xvii. 8. See on *v.* 18.

29. העץ. LXX adds διδύμου, καὶ ἦν ἐπὶ τοῦ ξύλου. An explanatory addition. LXX probably wished to indicate that ξύλου was not a tree but a stake on which to expose the body, with a cross-bar or second piece of wood at the top.

אל פתח שער העיר. LXX τὸν βόθρον = אל פחת. פחת was altered into פתח and the sentence filled out. A good example.

גדול. Not in LXX. Cf. x. 18.

31. בספר תורת. LXX omits ספר here and also in *v.* 34.

33. עמדים. Misread by LXX as עברים. The καὶ before οἱ ἱερεῖς seems firm, but A and Lucian omit the next καὶ of B.

33 end. Omit ישראל with LXX. This is shown to be right by the retention of the article in העם in M. T.

34. οὕτως. The Heb. ואחרי כן was read as ואחר, which means "and afterwards"; and כן was translated by οὕτως.

viii. 30—35 and ix. 1—2. Dillmann affirms that the position of viii. 30—35 in LXX after ix. 1—2 M. T. is due to wilful or capricious transposition. But this is to assume the point at issue. As against this, it is here suggested that the sections viii. 30—35 and ix. 1—2 are so to speak competitors for the more appropriate place. After viii. 29 there is a pause in the career of conquest. At this point, the statement that certain kings gathered together to oppose the victorious invaders comes in quite appropriately as narrating what happened upon the report of the conquest of Jericho and Ai.

Yet this pause in the action is also a good opportunity to introduce the narrative of the reading of the law. (One must of course, like the compiler himself, disregard the difficulty about the locality where the reading took place.)

If we take the LXX as representing the original order, it is quite possible that the Hebrew reviser preferred to give the reading of the law the better position at the expense of the short section ix. 1—2.

Steuernagel suggests that viii. 30—35 was a late addition, and was inserted in a different place in different MSS.

35. τοῖς ἀνδράσι in LXX is ampliative.

CHAPTER IX.

1. כל. Not in LXX. Inserted when the list was extended. In this chapter כל is absent from LXX in *v.* 5; in *v.* 19 M. T. has it twice, LXX once; B in one place and A in another. In *v.* 24 the first כל is absent from LXX. All this seems to display the hand of a reviser.

After מלכים LXX insert "the Amorites"; but as the Amorites are mentioned in the following list, the names of the various tribes are perhaps a subsequent addition, and LXX may represent the text in its intermediate stage, i.e. after the addition of the names of the tribes, and before the Hebrew reviser struck out the first mention of the Amorites.

Again, since M. T. includes the Girgashites in iii. 10 and xxiv. 11, the omission of the name here is probably accidental: LXX is given to completing the number in other passages. See Driver, *Deut.*, p. 97.

3. LXX gives יהוה for יהושע or rather ישוע. Probably the text was indistinct.

4. ἐπεσιτίσαντο is the exact translation of the right reading in M. T., but if we may judge from the rendering in *v.* 12 ἐφωδιάσθημεν, the original was ἡτοιμάσαντο and the exact translation a doublet.

ὤμων B is a corruption of ὄνων A.

5. LXX τὰ κοῖλα τῶν ὑποδημάτων αὐτῶν is a textual error for τὰ κοῖλα ὑποδήματα αὐτῶν = their boots. From Holmes and Parsons it appears that eight Greek MSS read κοῖλα τὰ ὑποδήματα, while

one, 44, has τὰ κοῖλα τὰ ὑποδήματα. Perhaps the Lyons Hept. which gives "calciamenta sua" had the right text. καὶ τὰ σανδάλια αὐτῶν is of course the doublet.

ὁ ἄρτος B, οἱ ἄρτοι A. Where A differs from M. T. it is probably right. Here it is upheld by B in *v.* 12. Hence read with many MSS ξηροὶ and βεβρωμένοι. *v.* 12 also shows that εὐρωτιῶν, which twelve MSS and the Lyons Heptateuch omit, is a doublet of βεβρωμένος.

7. חוי. LXX Χορραῖον. ו confused with ר.

8. מי. LXX πόθεν. A mistake.

9. שמעו. LXX τὸ ὄνομα may be a mistake induced by לשם of the preceding clause.

10. אשר בעשתרות. LXX ὃς κατῴκει ἐν Ἀσταρωθ καὶ ἐν Ἐδρασιν = אשר יושב. A case of confusion (almost haplography) between יושב and אשר. See on vi. 2.

11. καὶ ἀκούσαντες perhaps represents ויהי כשמעם; if so, ויאמר אל must be transposed to a later place in the sentence.

12. מבתינו. Not in LXX. If part of the original text, it is better taken after ביום צאתנו (Holzinger).

13. ואלה (2°). Omitted in LXX rightly. In accordance with the other sentences אשר would be required before בלו.

14. ויקחו האנשים. LXX ἄρχοντες. This is probably a deliberate alteration of LXX followed by the Peshitta. In the text as we have it the eating of the bread must have been entirely formal. The LXX perhaps saw the very plain difficulty of assuming that this formal act was done by the people at large, and ascribed it to the leaders.

פי. Omitted by LXX to avoid anthropomorphism, as also in xv. 13, xvii. 4, xix. 50, xxi. 3, xxii. 9.

15. לחיותם. Omit with Lucian. It is out of place here where the deception has not yet been discovered.

17. ביום השלישי. Not in LXX. Gilgal and Gibeon were only eighteen miles distant from one another: the length of time required is probably given correctly by the Hebrew reviser. Still, it may have been omitted by the translator since it occurs in the preceding verse.

וקרית יערים. LXX καὶ πόλεις Ἰαριν. For the same mistake see xv. 9, 60. In xviii. 14 it is taken as a proper name.

18. נשיאי עדה. LXX πάντες οἱ ἄρχοντες. Less definite: perhaps original.

20. והחיה. Infin. abs. Hiphil. LXX ζωγρῆσαι αὐτοὺς, καὶ περιποιησόμεθα αὐτούς. A doublet; but as ζωγρέω is used in ii. 13 and vi. 25 and περιποιέομαι in vi. 17 either might be the original. As ζωγρῆσαι must be the Aorist infin. active, it is possibly the addition of a grammarian who desired a parallel. Lyons Hept. did not have it, adservemus = περιποιησώμεθα; cf. the rendering in vi. 17. LXX and Lyons Hept. show that the ו is an addition; it is difficult to justify in M. T. in spite of Ewald 328 b. The sentence should run "This let us do: let us save them alive and so wrath shall not come upon us."

21. ויאמרו אליהם הנשיאים. Omit with LXX and Vulgate, and the sentence is much more vigorous. The next words will run יְחְיוּ וְיִהְיוּ, "Let them live, and let them be hewers of wood, etc." The pointing וַיִּהְיוּ became necessary after the omission in the last part of the verse.

After כל העדה most scholars read with F and numerous cursives ויעשו כל העדה. We might also prefix in accordance with 55 καὶ ἤρεσεν αὐτοῖς, וייטב בעיניהם.

22. τῶν κατοικούντων is the doublet, ἐνχώριοι the original.

23. עבד וחטבי עצים וגו׳. LXX A gives the purest text δοῦλος ξυλοκόπος = עבד חטב עצים. As the words are undoubtedly an insertion in the Hebrew from *v.* 21, it is possible that the full phrase had not yet been put in; or perhaps that the words were not in this verse at all when LXX was made, and that A has suffered less from correction than the other MSS.

לבית אלהי. Read with LXX לי ולאלהי; לבית became more appropriate after the centralisation of worship at Jerusalem. See the similar insertion of בית in vi. 24.

24. לעבדיך. LXX ἡμῖν as in *v.* 9; less courteous and therefore more original. Cf. 2 Samuel xviii. 29, Driver's note.

Before the words "and have done this thing" LXX, Lucian and several MSS in Holmes and Parsons add καὶ (ὡς) οὐχ ὑπελείφθη ἐν ἡμῖν πνεῦμα. The equivalent phrase in ii. 11, v. 1 and 1 Kings x. 5 is ולא קמה (or היה) בנו עוד רוח. ὑπελείφθη is not found in any rendering of the above three passages, but עמד is used in Haggai ii. 5 of the spirit, and in Josh. x. 8 עמד is translated by ὑπολείπω. The words may therefore have been in the Hebrew text. Lagarde, by bracketing καὶ ἐφοβήθημεν σφόδρα περὶ τῶν ψυχῶν ἡμῶν ἀπὸ προσώπου ὑμῶν, seems to regard ולא—רוח as the original and ונירא וגו׳ as a gloss. If we substitute

ולא עמדה בנו רוח for וניֵרא מאד לנפשתינו we get מפניכם at the end of the sentence in accordance with ii. 11 and v. 1.

26. LXX add Ἰησοῦς ἐν τῇ ἡμέρᾳ ἐκείνῃ; Ἰησοῦς is an explicit subject; the rest may represent the original or may have come in from below.

27. LXX B add διὰ τοῦτο ἐγένοντο κ.τ.λ. Dillmann rejects the words, but if there is a double account of the Gibeonite stratagem, there may well be a double subscription. Compare xix. 49—51, where there are two subscriptions to the account of the division of the land: JE, and P. The non-occurrence of πάσῃ τῇ συναγωγῇ = לכל עדה in the extra clause decides against P, i.e. it is not a mere repetition by the same hand. The omission could easily have arisen in M. T. by homoioteleuton; cf. מזבח יהוה.

CHAPTER X.

1. אדני צדק. LXX Ἀδωνιβεζέκ. The analogy of מלכי צדק Genesis xiv. is in favour of M. T.

עשה (twice). LXX ἐποίησαν (twice). There is no doubt that the singular is the right reading, but the instances are worth noting as upholding Lagarde's statement that final ה was often represented by a mark of abbreviation. If עשה had been written in full it could not have been translated by the plural. See also *vv.* 30, 32, 35.

השלימו. LXX ηὐτομόλησαν as in *v.* 4. The meaning of Hiphil "to make peace" was not known to the translator.

LXX has את יהושע before את ישראל. Judging from *v.* 4 this is correct. The eye of the scribe passed from the first את to the second.

ויהיו בקרבם. Omitted by LXX. It is better away.

2. All recensions of LXX agree in reading some case of αὐτὸς after ויִּראו. B ἀπ' αὐτῶν, A ἐν αὐτοῖς, Lucian ἐν αὐτοῖς. מהם may have been read before מאד.

כי עיר. Before כי עיר LXX read כי ידע. Most likely כי עיר was repeated and then עיר corrupted into or read as ידע.

וכי היא גדולה מן העי. Omit with LXX. LXX with its amplificatory tendency would not have left out this expression had it been in the text.

שרי הממלכה. LXX τῶν μητροπόλεων. M. T. = like one of the

royal cities. Gibeon had no king, but the city was as important as those that had. LXX perhaps read הָאֻמּוֹת; see xiv. 15, xv. 13 and Moore's *Judges*, p. 25.

5. LXX omit יאספו perhaps accidentally. LXX Jebusites for Amorites.

10. בית חורן. LXX Ὡρωνειν = חרנים also next verse.

10, 11. LXX read בני in both verses after לפני *v.* 10 and מפני *v.* 11 perhaps rightly. The word could easily have fallen out.

11. גדולת. LXX χαλάζης = ברד. This may be right. ברד is definite in the Hebrew in the next clause.

וימתו. LXX omit rightly and begin the next sentence with ויהיו. When ויהיו was corrupted into וימתו it was joined to the preceding sentence.

ἐν τῷ πολέμῳ. Ampliative.

12. M. T. omits several words found in LXX; and LXX omits two words found in M. T., after "the Amorite." LXX has ὑποχείριον Ἰσραηλ ἡνίκα συνέτριψεν αὐτοὺς ἐν Γαβαων καὶ συνετρίβησαν ἀπὸ προσώπου υἱῶν Ἰσραηλ. A and Lucian omit υἱῶν.

LXX = ביד ישראל כי הכם בגבען ויכו לפני (בני) ישראל. The omission in M. T. is no doubt due to the resemblance between ביד ישראל and בני ישראל. It is noticeable that if we adopt LXX insertion and omission, we drop the Deuteronomic phrase נתן לפני so that 12 a can be restored to JE which would then run from 9 to 14 a.

לעיני ישראל. Not in LXX. Mr Thackeray, *J. T. S.* vol. XI. p. 528, argues that these words are the corruption of a gloss לבני ישראל later than LXX.

13. גוי. LXX ὁ Θεός = יהוה as often in LXX, eleven times in this book. LXX seems preferable, in view of the interposition of Jehovah recorded in *v.* 11. The form (see chapter iv. 5) used for the tetragrammaton would be the single letter ו with some mark of abbreviation. This would easily be corrupted into גוי. In viii. 8 יהוה and הזה are confused. Mr Thackeray suggests that the Massorites deliberately altered יהוה into גוי, but a reviser would surely have written הגוי.

הלא היא כתובה על ספר הישר. Omitted by LXX BA. There certainly seems to be no reason for LXX omitting this if it had been in their text. Moreover Mr Thackeray (*op. cit.*) has made it very probable that the words are an insertion subsequent to LXX.

14. בקול omitted here and in v. 6 by LXX, no doubt to avoid anthropomorphism.

15. Omitted in LXX together with *v.* 43. Bennett's suggestion that *v.* 15 was omitted purposely to avoid the contradiction in *v.* 21 might hold if LXX contained *v.* 43. See Introduction, p. 4.

18. גדלות. Omit with LXX. The same omission here and in *v.* 27 is almost conclusive.

20. ובני. LXX B καὶ πᾶς υἱός. An amplification.

מהם ויבאו. The omission of these words with LXX BA enables the right meaning "flee for refuge" to be given to שרדו. Bennett's emendation is not at all satisfactory. השרדים (מהם) באו. It is a conjectural emendation where a various reading exists which gives perfectly good sense. "The fugitives fled for refuge to the fortified cities."

21. אל המחנה. "To the camp to Joshua at Maqqedah" is improved by the omission of the first two words with LXX.

חרץ. ἔγρυξεν. LXX did not know the word, and as a consequence mistranslated the sentence.

לאיש. Omit ל with LXX. A case of dittography.

22. אלי in this verse and אליו in 23 are not represented in LXX. They may possibly have been omitted as unnecessary; as may also be the case with את פי before "the cave" here and in *v.* 27.

23. ויעשו כן. Omitted in LXX BA. Most probably an insertion of a scribe; but as ויהי is often omitted (see next verse) as superfluous, it is just possible that the translator treated ויעשו כן in the same way. But the similar omission in *v.* 15 supports LXX.

24. LXX omit המלכים האלה twice: probably a gloss in both places, see Intro., p. 5.

ויאמר אל קציני. LXX omit ויאמר אל and have λέγων αὐτοῖς before "Come near." This suggests that the text has suffered some alteration. The five words before קרבו are not above suspicion. They include קצין in the plural and הֶהָלְכוּא, both of which call for notice. קצין is used nowhere else in the Hexateuch and from its use in Judges xi. 6 is plainly inappropriate here; Joshua himself is the קצין. Further from ch. viii. we see that the Elders would be the people whom Joshua would call. Again ההלכוא is a very late construction—see Ges. Kautzsch 138 i, and for the א see 23 i,—and in addition the expression is not in the style of the writer whose phraseology in ch. viii. would lead us to expect simply אשר אִתּוֹ; i.e. ההלכוא is not only impossible in an early writer but is not likely to be the phrase which this writer would use. From this we may infer that the five words are not the original text which may have run "And Joshua called to all Israel and the Elders who were with him" and that at the time of the LXX translation the augmented text had not yet been fully accommodated to its surroundings. For another case where LXX represents an intermediate state of the text see iii. 13.

26. LXX omit אחרי כן וימיתם. The words are an addition of a scribe who thought that ויכם did not necessarily include death and that it was better to be quite explicit.

27. גדולות. Omit with LXX: see *v.* 18.

פי. Not in LXX: see on *v.* 22.

28. LXX add καὶ διαπεφευγὼς = ופליט. So in *vv.* 30 and 33. This may be an addition by LXX following viii. 22, but it may also be an example of the Hebrew reviser seeking uniformity by omission as he does elsewhere in this chapter by insertion. See on *v.* 35.

ואת מלכה. Not in LXX. Considerations of style are unfavourable to the words (see Driver on 1 *Samuel* v. 10). According to Dr Driver this construction occurs only eleven or twelve times in the O.T. Six of these are in this chapter. If we may go by the LXX two of the instances (28 and 32) are due to a reviser subsequent to LXX.

כל הנפש. LXX πᾶν ἐμπνέον = כל הנשמה. See Intro., p. 7, and Carpenter and Battersby *in loco.*

30. After ביד ישראל LXX supply וילכדה as in *v.* 32.

32. ואת כל הנפש אשר בה. LXX reads καὶ ἐξωλέθρευσεν αὐτὴν = החרים אתה as in *v.* 28.

35. ואת כל הנפש וגו' was inserted by the Hebrew reviser for the sake of uniformity with *vv.* 28, 30, 35, 37. No doubt *vv.* 28 and 32 LXX give the original form of the sentence in normal Hebrew.

37. ואת מלכה ואת כל עריה. This is one of the passages where Dillmann alleges deliberate omission. The King of Hebron has already been slain in *v.* 26, therefore the translator omitted the statement here. But if so, why were the three following

words omitted also? It is probably an anticipatory insertion from *v.* 39.

38. וילחם. LXX = ויחן probably under influence of *v.* 31.

41. "And Joshua smote them." Omit with LXX. The sentence should begin with 40b ואת כל "and all that breathed he devoted, from K. Barnea to Gaza."

42. לכד. LXX ἐπάταξεν = הכה. M. T. is probably the correction of a Hebrew scribe who thought that ארץ required לכד, but *v.* 40 decides otherwise.

43. To be omitted with LXX as *v.* 15.

CHAPTER XI.

2. מצפון. LXX read צדון and amplified by μεγάλην from *v.* 8.

נגב. LXX = נגד an easy mistake if it is one.

נפת. By metathesis LXX read פנת and joined it to the next word; hence Φενναεδδωρ. They also divided the sentence wrongly, taking מים at the beginning of *v.* 3, showing at the same time that they did not know that מים meant westward.

3. The Hittites and the Hivites should change places in M. T., so LXX.

Hermon. LXX τὸν ἔρημον. After transliteration Ερμον was corrupted into a common Greek word. Cf. Amos iii. 12 where ערש is represented by ἱερεῖς.

4. מחניהם. LXX βασιλεῖς. Confusion of ח and ל.

עם רב omitted by LXX. Probably not in the original.

6. חללים. LXX τετροπωμένους. In xiii. 22 practically the same mistake is made. LXX generally represents חלל by τραυματίας "a wounded man," and as that would not be suitable here the translator guessed.

7. LXX add ἐν τῇ ὀρεινῇ = בהר, a corrupt repetition of בהם.

10. הכה בחרב. Omitted by LXX. The translator's eye passed from the last כ of מלכה, the ה not being written, to the כ of כי. The Hebrew reviser would not have inserted a neat circumstantial clause like this: cf. viii. 13 where he makes an original circumstantial clause into an objective clause עקבו.

13. עמדות על תלם. LXX κεχωματισμένα. The translator seems to have coined a word. Perhaps the assonance with חומה had something to do with it. Delete the last word in 13, 'Joshua';

in LXX Israel. A good example of the truth of Wellhausen's canon "where M. T. and LXX differ in respect of a subject it is probable that the original text had neither."

14. LXX read "all its spoil" referring to Hazor. This is probably right as *vv.* 13 b and 14 refer to Hazor only.

16. LXX add πρὸς τῷ ὄρει, probably a corrupt repetition of the following words.

19. The meaning of השלים "to make peace with" was not known to LXX. In x. 1 and 4 it is rendered by αὐτομολέω, here by οὐ λαμβάνω. A and F give παρέδωκεν, an Aramaism.

20. בלתי וגו׳. Omit with LXX. The original writer was not so minutely accurate.

21. הר. LXX γένους, reading perhaps according to an old conjecture דר.

22. בארץ. Omit with LXX. The expression "land of the children of Israel" does not seem to occur. In xxi. 41 'possession' of the children of Israel is rendered.

CHAPTER XII.

In *v.* 2 LXX B substitutes Arnon for Aroer and consequently omits Arnon from its proper place; it also has μέρος for μέσον. The same phrase is translated quite correctly in xiii. 9.

2. יבק הנחל. This peculiar phrase occurs also in Deut. iii. 16. הנחל is omitted by LXX B, A, F here, but is found in Deut. iii. 16. The fact that יבק occurs elsewhere by itself without נחל is on the side of the LXX.

4. גבול. Omit with LXX. עוג is parallel to סיחון in *v.* 2.

5. ומשל. Omit ו with LXX. משל as in *v.* 2. That after גלעד עד has fallen out is confirmed by Lucian.

7. הארץ. LXX = Amorites, shown to be original by x. 5.

9—24. אחד. Omitted by B, A, F, inserted in Lucian which has been accommodated all through this list to a text very little different from M. T.

18. LXX Ὀφεκ τῆς Ἀρωκ. Ἀρωκ was originally Σαρωκ, but lost the Σ by haplography. M. T. is emended by all moderns on the basis of this to אפק לשרון.

19. מדון is omitted here by LXX B, A, F but probably turns up in the next verse.

20. שמרון מראון. LXX שמעון, omitting מראון directly after שמעון and giving βασιλέα Μαμρωθ as the next king. See Dr Driver's note in Kittel.

23. לגלגל. LXX τῆς Γαλειλαίας = לגליל which is generally accepted.

24. M. T. 31 kings. LXX 29 (Ἀιραθ and Ἀραθ in 14 are doublets). These numbers show editing on both sides as no doubt M. T. list must be reduced to 30 and LXX list raised to 30. It is generally agreed that in *v.* 18 M. T. one king is to be read instead of two: there does not seem to be the same agreement as to which king LXX omitted. Dillmann and Bennett say Maqqedah, Carpenter and Battersby, Madon; but Bethel *v.* 16 is the one omitted. Maqqedah is represented by Ηλαδ which is certainly a bad corruption of Μακηδα, but the Lyons Hept. has "regem Odolla, regem Mageda, regem Iafud"; the omission of Bethel and the form Iafud show that this is not from a corrected text. Madon or its equivalent turns up in LXX in *v.* 20.

CHAPTER XIII.

3 and 4. The M. T. has put the soph pasuq at the wrong word. The stop is put at the right word in the Peshitta. But LXX also took the words in the right connection. The comma in Swete at τῷ Ευαιῳ is a plain instance of the LXX verse-numbering being governed by that of the Hebrew Bible. That ἐκ Θαιμαν must go with τῷ Ευαιῳ is proved by the καὶ which follows, which is also represented in the Peshitta, so that we must read וכל ארץ.

4 b. ומערה אשר לצידונים. LXX ἐναντίον (Lucian ἀπὸ) Γαζης. Lyons Heptateuch "a Gaza."

On the basis of LXX and Deut. ii. 23 we may perhaps restore the right reading here. The LXX read מעזה והצידונים. The waw before הצידונים may represent the ד of עד which would partly explain the אשר of M. T. so that the true reading may have been "From Gaza to the Zidonians." Deut. ii. 23 speaks of the Avvim who dwelt in villages as far as Gaza. The mention of Gaza after the Avvim here would therefore be natural. The writer wished to denote a large extent of country from the South to the North "all the land of the Canaanites"; the phrase "from Gaza to the Zidonians" does this. The waw before מערה in M. T. is a dittograph from the preceding letter.

5. הנבלי. LXX Γαλιαθ. Some ingenious scribe thinking of Goliath of Gath added the word φυλιστιειμ.

6. בנחלה. LXX translation by ἐν shows ignorance of ב essentiae, see xxiii. 4.

7 and 8. The M. T. here is confessedly imperfect. The LXX translated the true text but subsequently suffered from interpolation as is seen when the passage is turned into Hebrew.

וחצי שבט מנשה׃ 8 מהירדן עד הים הגדול מבוא השמש תתן אתה הים
הגדול ונבול׃ לשני השבטים וחצי שבט מנשה (הראובני והגדי) נתן משה
נחלה בעבר הירדן מזרחה׃ נתן להם משה עבד יהוה מערושר וגו׳

The eye of the Hebrew scribe passed over the fourteen words between שבט מנשה at the end of *v.* 7 to their second occurrence later on. Again the words הראובני והגדי were not in the text before the LXX. It was only after the omission had taken place in M. T. that they were required in that text to make good the omission. After their insertion in M. T. they were transferred to the LXX.

Dillmann's statement therefore that the LXX cannot be the *original* text because of the insertion of τῷ Ρ. καὶ τῷ Γ. is true, but does not, as he thinks, discredit the LXX. The LXX as we have it is not the original it is true, but only because it contains an interpolation; when this is banished, it does represent the original. Hollenberg's argument that if the LXX translator had inserted the words τῷ Ρ. καὶ τῷ Γ. they would not appear in such an awkward place holds good but his conclusion that they were therefore in the text before LXX does not.

The process then by which M. T. obtained its present form was (1) omission by homoioteleuton, (2) filling out of text by the insertion of the first six words in *v.* 8 and כאשר later on.

9. מידבא עד דיבן. LXX has ἀπὸ Δαιδαβαν which may be the remnant of the full expression.

10. LXX add καὶ τὸν Χαναναῖον, probably an explanatory gloss.

13. LXX insert Βασιλεὺς before גשור. The translator may have considered that as הגשורי represented the people גשור by itself could not.

14 b. LXX καὶ οὗτος ὁ καταμερισμὸς ὃν κατεμέρισε Μωυσης τοῖς

υἱοῖς Ἰσραηλ ἐν Ἀραβωθ Μωαβ κ.τ.λ. The genuineness of this clause, which does not appear in the Hebrew, is generally accepted: no doubt it is guaranteed by the transliteration of P's phrase Ἀραβωθ Μωαβ. But it seems impossible to admit that καταμερισμός represents a Hebrew word before the translator. It is never used elsewhere in the LXX. The verb καταμερίζω is also very rare and requires explaining as a translation of נחל. Μερίζω it is true is used, but it represents חלק in xiii. 7, xiv. 5 and no doubt in xviii. 6. The translation is therefore unique.

The most probable explanation seems to be that the superscription was אלה אשר נחל as in *v.* 32 and that אלה was read as וזה, the confusion of ו and א being very frequent. וזה was naturally translated by καὶ οὗτος. As there was no substantive before אשר the translator *supplied* one by καταμερισμός; having supplied it he not unnaturally continued with the cognate verb καταμερίζω for נחל although he had translated נחלה in the previous clause by κληρονομία. A translator without a Hebrew word before him was liable to use a Greek word which betrays the absence of a Hebrew original. This is seen here and also in κείμενον in iv. 6 and συντελεία and διάβασις in iv. 8.

15. למטה בני ראובן. τῇ φυλῇ Ρουβην. Hollenberg compares xiii. 24, xv. 1, xviii. 21, xix. 1, 17, 24, 40 and calls them instances of simplification; but the enumeration is incomplete, and investigation of all the similar passages throws doubt on this theory of simplification, see xix. 1.

16, 17. Both LXX and Peshitta make the sentence end at Heshbon.

21. LXX omits אשר מלך בחשבון. The repetition of אשר would account for this.

נסיכי סיחון. LXX ἄρχοντα ἔναρα. Schleusner's conjecture ἄρχοντας παρά is most ingenious, but Hollenberg is probably right in regarding ἄρχοντα and ἔναρα as doublets; ἔναρα being the original word. נסיך is very rare; it occurs only four times in O.T. LXX no doubt guessed. ἔναρα is found nowhere else in the Greek Bible.

22. בני ישראל בחרב. Omit with LXX BA. "Children of Israel" is an explicit subject, "with the sword" a scribal insertion.

אל חלליהם. Hollenberg's emendation of ῥοπῇ into τροπῇ is confirmed by Lucian.

23. ו of ונבול is omitted by LXX, see *v.* 27. Note the preceding ו.

24. LXX = בני גד, Peshitta למטה גד, M. T. has both, see note on *v.* 15.

26. לדבר. ל is a dittograph; not in LXX.

27. ונבול. LXX ὁριεῖ reading יגבול, but as the verb in the few instances in which it occurs is transitive, M. T. is to be preferred; see also on xv. 47.

28. LXX add αὐχένα ἐπιστρέψουσιν ἐναντίον τῶν ἐχθρῶν αὐτῶν = ערף יפנו לפני איביהם. A reason for these words in their present form is difficult to find. Why should the *defeat* of Gad be alluded to? Can it be that the Hebrew, no doubt originally a marginal gloss, was misread by LXX and was originally ערף יפנו לפניהם איביהם? A mention of the prowess of Gad would not be unnatural: no other members of a tribe are spoken of in the same way as those of Gad are in 1 Chron. xii. 8—15.

> "Mighty men of valour trained for war—whose faces were like the faces of lions—swift as the roes upon the mountains." Of the captains "the least was equal to a hundred and the greatest to a thousand."

The misreading would be helped by the fact that in incorporating the gloss into the text, the translator by inserting ὅτι ἐγενήθη could give a reason for the defeat of the Gadites.

29. ויהי לחצי וגו׳. Plainly a doublet. Not in LXX.

32. πέραν τοῦ Ἰορδάνου the same insertion as in v. 10. Lyons Hept. has it here and not in v. 10.

33. Omit with LXX. Duplicate of 14.

CHAPTER XIV.

2. בגורל נחלתם. Dillmann notices the unsatisfactoriness of translating "by the lot of their inheritance," and also mentions that LXX and Targum translate as though they had a verb before them.

Hence the acceptability of Dr Driver's emendation בגורל נחלו אתם. Perhaps we must also with Peshitta read לתת after משה. LXX יהושע.

3. כי נתן–המטה. Omitted in LXX perhaps by homoioteleuton.

8. המסיו. In Deut. i. 28 המסו. LXX here μετέστησαν. In Deut. ἀπέστησαν. A guess in both places. Yet ii. 11, v. 1 and vii. 5 show that the Niphal was known.

12. τὸ ῥῆμα τοῦτο. Explanatory insertion by LXX.

What is it that Joshua is said to have heard? The promise made to Caleb? or the fact that the Anakim dwelt in Hebron? The LXX and Vulgate readings give the first interpretation, the Hebrew allows either. We may get some help from the Hebrew by the consideration that the pronoun אתה before שמעת must have some emphasis (Driver, *Tenses*, § 160, Ob.). This seems to confirm the LXX and the Vulgate "Thou thyself didst hear the promise made. You have not to take my mere assertion." Here we have some reason for an emphatic אתה. If the second interpretation is taken אתה remains without any emphasis. "Thou thyself didst hear that the Anakim dwell there" would be pointless. There was no need to remind Joshua that he had heard 40 years ago what he now would know without doubt.

LXX did not seem to know the meaning of אולי. Here we get ἐὰν, in ix. 7 ὅρα μή, Gen. xvi. 2 ἵνα, xviii. 24 ἐὰν δέ, xxiv. 5 μή ποτε, 1 Sam. vi. 5, ix. 6 ὅπως.

אשר. LXX καθά = כאשר perhaps rightly, cf. the last three words of the verse.

13. υἱῷ Κενεζ in LXX is probably a later insertion. In *vv.* 6 and 14 we get ὁ Κενεζαιος. The LXX readings are confused and the expression is absent from the Lyons Heptateuch.

15. האדם הגדול וגו׳. LXX μητρόπολις = אם mother city. The correction is as old as Schleusner; see x. 2.

CHAPTER XV.

In the description of the boundaries which is given in cc. xv.—xix., we should expect παραπορεύομαι for עבר and περιπορεύομαι for סבב. We may assume that the translator knew the meaning of these simple words and rendered them correctly. We may therefore certainly infer that where we get περιπορεύομαι for עבר as in xv. 3 and xix. 13, and παραπορεύομαι for סבב as in xviii. 14, the Greek text has suffered corruption.

But there are other cases where the Greek renderings lead one to suspect, not corruption of the Greek text, but Hebrew editorial alteration. It seems hardly likely that the Greek translator would have been so inconsistent as to give διεκβάλλω for יצא in xv. 4, 11 *bis*, and the same word for עבר in xv. 7: or διελεύσεται for עבר in xviii. 13 and 18, and the same word for יצא in xviii. 15, xix. 12, 27 and 34.

The following are the renderings of יצא and עבר and סבב according to our present texts.

יצא. διαπορεύομαι xv. 3, διεκβάλλω xv. 4, 11 *bis*, xvi. 7, ἐξέρχομαι xvi. 2, xviii. 11, ἔρχομαι xvi. 1, διέρχομαι xviii. 15, xix. 12, 27, 34, παρέρχομαι xviii. 17.

עבר. ἐκπεριπορεύομαι xv. 3, ἐκπορεύομαι xv. 3, 4, παραπορεύομαι xv. 6, 10, διεκβάλλω xv. 7, παρέρχομαι xv. 11, xvi. 2, 6, διέρχομαι xviii. 13, 18, περιέρχομαι xix. 13.

סבב. ἐκπορεύομαι xv. 3, περιέρχομαι xv. 10, xvi. 6, xix. 14, παρέρχομαι xviii. 14.

1. ויהי הגורל. LXX = הגבול, so in xvi. 1 and xvii. 1. M. T. undoubtedly deserves the preference especially in view of xxi. 38 "their allotted portion was twelve cities," where the LXX is certainly wrong. But M. T. is not consistent, having in xvi. 1 ויצא הגורל and in the other two places ויהי הגורל. In xvi. 1 LXX καὶ ἐγένετο is no doubt right. ויצא may be the alteration of a scribe who like the Greek translator did not realise the meaning of גורל as "an allotted portion" which it has with ויהי. The mistake was, of course, facilitated by the resemblance between נבל and גרל. ἕως Καδης. Probably LXX misread קצה as קדש and translated only one of the expressions meaning Southward.

3. אדרה. LXX εἰς Σαραδα for εἰς Ἀραδα. Reverse mistake of τῆς Ἀρωκ for τῆς Σαρωκ xii. 18, see νάπης Σονναμ in xviii. 16.

5. קצה (1°). Omitted by LXX though it is translated on its second occurrence in the verse.

7. וצפונה פנה. LXX has here καταβαίνει which = וירד. By common consent פנה is impossible. If this is struck out as a dittograph (Ehrlich) we have וצפונה to account for. But if we are to go by the respective positions of the valley of Achor, Adummim and En-shemesh, the mention of a northward direction is not likely. Steuernagel would take וצפונה as a corruption of ופנה; Ehrlich's objection to this, that פנה is never used elsewhere of boundaries, fails in view of the fact that הלך also is so used only once (xvii. 7). ופנה may have been misread by LXX.

ועבר הגבול. LXX καὶ διεκβάλλει = ויצא. May be the alteration of Hebrew reviser.

8. Valley of Rephaim. LXX = 'land' perhaps rightly, cf. Deut. ii. 20, iii. 13.

9. ערי. Omitted by LXX. Probably a dittograph of הר.

10. ועבר comes earlier in LXX. הר יערים. LXX = עיר.

11. ὅρια ἐπὶ λίβα. Textual error for ἐπὶ ὄρος Βαλα.

13. אב. LXX μητρόπολις = אם. See x. 2.

14. ילידי הענק. Not in LXX. The phrase is both superfluous and inaccurate. The right phrase בני הענק has occurred immediately before.

16. ἐκκόψῃ is the doublet. It is omitted by nearly 30 MSS. and the Lyons Hept. LXX misread יכה as לכד and translated by the usual word, λαμβάνω. The translation of the second לכד was accordingly varied by κυριεύω.

18. ותסיתהו. LXX BA and Lucian συνεβουλεύσατο αὐτῷ λέγουσα Αἰτήσομαι τὸν πατέρα μου. According to Holmes and Parsons, seven or eight MSS. read συνεβούλευσεν αὐτῇ λέγων, Αἴτησαι τὸν πατέρα σου. This is confirmed by the corresponding passage in Judges i. 14 LXX, where M. T. has suffered in the same way as here. We must therefore read וַיְסִיתֶהָ. Lyons Hept. perhaps had the whole passage right. Et factum est cum introiret ad eam, consilium dedit illi dicens: Pete a patre tuo.

ותצנח. LXX did not know the word and gives ἐβόησεν. It may possibly have been read as ותצעק, see xxiv. 7.

19. גלת מים. LXX takes as a proper name; though in B there must have been considerable corruption before τὴν Βοθθανεις and τὴν Γοναιθλαν could represent the same word.

Recent scholars have adopted Moore's suggestion on Judges i. 15 that the true reading is Gullath maim, Gullath illith and Gullath taḥtith. It is true that Gulloth is not in itself impossible, *vide* "Succoth": but in favour of Gullath we have,

(1) Γωλαθμαιμ in LXX A in Joshua, and λύτρωσιν in Judges, showing that the word was taken to be the singular, not the plural form.

(2) The fact that the adjectives are taken as singular in LXX both in Joshua and Judges, and also in M. T. of Judges, i.e. the LXX both in Joshua and Judges support Gullath while M. T. does so in Judges.

21. הערים מקצה. LXX πόλεις αὐτῶν πόλεις πρός. The translation of מקצה would be ἀπὸ μέρους, when the α of ἀπό was lost ΠΟΜΕΡΟΥΣ became ΠΟΛΙΣΠΡΟΣ.

בנגבה. LXX ἐπὶ τῆς ἐρήμου. An Aramaism.

22. ועדעדה. LXX B Ἀρουηλ, 120 Ἀρουηρ = ערער or ערערה, see Driver, *Samuel*, p. 226. The reading Ἀδαδα in A, Lucian etc. is a very clear example of the alteration of the original LXX text to agree with M. T.

25. חצור חדתה. The adjective is not represented in LXX. It looks like a late gloss, as if the חצור mentioned in the text had been destroyed and a new town built. חצור appears as αἱ κῶμαι αὐτῶν = חצריהן. If חדתה was indistinct it may have been taken for a suffix. קריות appears as αἱ πόλεις. The translator took it as a plural of קריה, not knowing that the plural form was not in use. See the same mistake in xviii. 28 etc.

28. ובזיותיה. All moderns read with LXX ובנותיה.

30. כסיל. LXX Βαιθηλ, combined with xix. 4, shows that the right reading is בתול or rather ביתאל. For the place see Driver's note on 1 *Sam.* xxx. 27.

32. Both M. T. and LXX agree that there should be 29 names; both also are inconsistent: LXX gives 30, M. T. 36. It is generally considered that four names have been inserted in M. T. here from Nehemiah xi. 27—28, but as these four names are in LXX the text must have suffered interpolation at an early date, and LXX can therefore afford no help in determining which cities should be omitted.

46. וימה. LXX, Γεμνα, take it as a proper name. The text no doubt was indistinct.

47. All the versions represent גדול, but M. T. Kethib גבול is difficult to explain: see Gray's *Numbers*, xxxiv. 6. In accordance with Haupt's suggestion, the translation of this passage would be "the sea being the border and its adjacent territory."

59. Eleven additional names in LXX are generally accepted.

61. במדבר. LXX Βαδδαργεις, a corruption of the transliteration. After the corruption had taken place, the word was taken as a proper name and ἑπτά substituted for ἕξ in the next verse.

62. עיר המלח. LXX B πόλεις Σαδων, Lucian τῶν ἁλῶν, Lyons Heptateuch, civitates allon.

63. את בני יהודה. Not in LXX.

CHAPTER XVI.

1. ויצא הגורל. LXX read ויהי. See on xv. 1.

למי יריחו. Not in LXX. Holzinger affirms that the expression was deliberately left out by the translator. But it is not easy to think that our translator would have found any difficulty in the words. They look like a doublet.

המדבר. LXX καὶ ἀναβήσεται κ.τ.λ. המדבר may originally have been a corrupt repetition of מזרחה. τὴν ἔρημον looks like a late insertion in LXX. The LXX obviously gives the better text. Dillmann admits that the syntax of המדבר is doubtful and that עלה should have the article. Moreover the LXX is confirmed by xviii. 12 b as pointed out by Dr Driver. LXX is accepted by Steuernagel and Dr Driver. Read ועלה מיריחו בהר.

2. ארכי עטרות. In B Χαταρωθει. The Χ is the sole remnant of Αρχι.

3. וירד is another confirmation of the LXX reading ועלה in *v.* 1. LXX διελεύσεται shows careless translation, though in *v.* 2 the words are quite accurately rendered.

LXX omits ועד גזר. It appears at the end of *v.* 5.

6. המכמתת. Neither M. T. nor LXX gives a satisfactory meaning. According to *Ency. Bib.* no emendation of the text has been proposed. Dr Driver suggests insertion of ויהי גבולם. Steuernagel inserts "und die Grenze läuft aus nach dem Meere zu." Omit אותו with LXX.

7. LXX omits וירד and translates נערתה by κῶμαι as though it were pointed נַעֲרֹתֶיהָ.

8. נחל קנה. LXX χελκανα.

10. ἕως ἀνέβη Φαραω......καὶ τοὺς κατοικοῦντας ἐν Γαζερ ἐξεκέντησαν· καὶ ἔδωκεν αὐτὴν Φαραω ἐν φερνῇ τῇ θυγατρὶ αὐτοῦ. Hollenberg and Dillmann take this verse, which comes in the LXX after ἕως τῆς ἡμέρας ταύτης, as an insertion from 1 Kings ix. 16. But against this must be set:

(1) The circumstance that the passage in 1 Kings ix. 16 M. T. appears in LXX B and Lucian as iv. 32. A wandering passage in Kings has no claim to be considered the original of the passage here.

(2) The fact that LXX here does not render the clause ויהי למס עבד: which indeed is not consistent with LXX reading.

If the Canaanites in Gezer had been reduced למס there would have been no necessity for Pharaoh's expedition.

(3) The presence of a short clause in the Hebrew instead of the long clause given in LXX, which suggests abbreviation; an indisputable example of abbreviation of this kind is found in 1 Sam. xxxi. 6, 7 compared with 1 Chron. x. See Driver *in loco.*

There are also three linguistic points in favour of LXX here.

(1) The passage in LXX Kings does not contain a translation of הרג in B or Lucian, and in A ἀποκτείνω is used.

(2) φερνή is used here, ἀποστολαί in Kings.

(3) The ב essentiae is absent from Kings and is probably represented here by ἐν.

The translation of הרג by the rare word ἐκκεντέω is not against the genuineness of the passage. It is used in Numbers xxii. 29 to translate הרג and our translator was not averse to rare words; cf. κατορύσσω for burying, in xxiv. 32 and 33 instead of θάπτω, and in xxiii. 12 we get another rare word in συγκαταμίγνυμι.

Again, if the ἐν in ἐν φερνῇ represents the ב essentiae, this is a strong point in favour of a Hebrew original; cf. Josh. xiii. 6 and 7 and xxiii. 4 where the ב essentiae though misunderstood is rendered by ἐν. In the passage in Kings שלחים is used without ב.

The Hebrew reviser no doubt objected to the statement that Gezer kept its independence till the time of Solomon and accordingly omitted the passage. It should be added that the words ἕως τῆς ἡμέρας ταύτης can have been no part of the original LXX and one MS, 44, omits them.

CHAPTER XVII.

2. בני מנשה בן יוסף. Omitted in LXX. The fact that in the next verse LXX omits בן גלעד בן מכיר בן מנשה makes it probable that these are both later additions.

5. הבשן. Not in LXX.

5 a. LXX here quite misunderstood the text.

מנשה עשרה לבד. This is represented by ἀπὸ Ἀνασσα καὶ πεδίον Λαβεκ, i.e. עשרה was read ושדה and לבד was transliterated.

7. Δηλαναθ ἥ ἐστι κατὰ πρόσωπον υἱῶν ᾽Αναθ. LXX again misunderstood the text. In the first part Δηλαναθ for מאשר המכמתת seems to defy explanation. The two names were probably taken as one, and textual corruption did the rest. For the other words it may be suggested that על פני שכם was read על בני שנט = κατὰ υἱοὺς Σαναθ. The Σ of Σαναθ was dropped after the final σ of υἱοὺς as elsewhere and became κατὰ υἱοὺς ᾽Αναθ. This was subsequently emended by the insertion of πρόσωπον to render פני. Hence κατὰ πρόσωπον υἱῶν ᾽Αναθ,—υἱῶν for the sake of grammar.

8. למנשה היתה ארץ תפוח. LXX = למנשה יהיה. LXX is probably right. עין תפוח was repeated to emphasise the fact that the spring belonged to Manasseh but Tappuach to Ephraim. Subsequently עין was corrupted into ארץ. Interchange of א and ע is frequent, י or ו is confused with ר in this book, see ix. 7. For and ץ see Graetz, *die Psalmen*, p. 129.

9. LXX Ἰαριηλ is a strange reading but ערים האלה is not above suspicion. A subsequent reviser added τερέμινθος as a translation of האלה. LXX καὶ ἔσται = והיה = והיו.

11. In this verse LXX omits all mention of Ibleam, Endor, and Taanach; and amplifies after נפת. Since שלשת in M.T. means 'a triad of,' this justifies the three names in LXX, Bethshean, Dor and Megiddo; especially as LXX did not understand the word שלשת in this sense, but took it to mean 'a third,' a fact which seems to negative Dillmann's suggestion that LXX reduced the names to three on account of שלשת. We may conjecture that after the original text was written, the two names Ibleam and Taanach were inserted from Judges i. 27. Endor is perhaps a corrupt repetition of Dor. This would account for the six names in M. T. The fourfold ישבי is admittedly an insertion from Judges, two instances of which got into LXX here as τοὺς κατοικοῦντας ἐπὶ τοὺς κ. and οἱ κατοικοῦντες.

14. עד אשר עד כה. LXX has καί, and the sentence reads better as they give it, "seeing I am a great people and J. hath blessed me." The Vulgate agrees with LXX, and is plainly not dependent on the old Latin.

15. שם בארץ הפרזי והרפאים. LXX omits. The phrase may be due to an endeavour to localise the new territory.

16. ἀρέσκει, textual corruption for ἀρκέσει.

17. בית יוסף. LXX gives υἱοί under the influence of *v.* 14.

The alteration may have been intentional, but בני and בית would not differ much in the exemplar. Omit "to Ephraim and to Manasseh" with LXX.

18. תצאתיו. Omitted by LXX which is supported by והיה Kthib.

כי חזק הוא. LXX = כי חזקת ממנו which suits the context better. So Dr Driver.

CHAPTER XVIII.

3. This chapter exhibits undoubted traces of the hand of the reviser, otherwise one would be inclined to think the omission of לבוא before לרשת to be an abbreviation.

אבותיכם. "J′, the God of your fathers" occurs nowhere else in this book, whereas "J′, your God" or "our God" occurs several times in Joshua's speeches; see *v.* 6. Perhaps therefore LXX "J′, our God" is right. Cf. note on xxiv. 14 and 15.

4. ואשלחם. Omit with LXX. The sentence runs better without it.

לפי נחלתם וגו'. LXX ἐναντίον μου is a doublet.

The translator first went wrong over לפי נחלתם. This he translated by καθὰ δεήσει διελεῖν αὐτήν. This may pass as not absolutely misleading. The remainder of the sentence he rendered unintelligently: he forgot that it was a command and made it a narrative. Instead of "and let them come (or perhaps bring it) to me, and let them divide it into seven parts" he gives "and they came to him, and he divided it into seven parts." The Hebrew text in the script before the translator with a misreading of one letter can quite easily bear this meaning. Nothing but an intelligent appreciation of the context could have kept him right.

6. פֹּה. Omit with LXX G, some cursives, the Syro-Hex. and the Lyons Heptateuch.

תכתבו. LXX μερίσατε = יחלקו. This deviation is to be compared with that in *v.* 8 where לכתב is rendered by χωροβατῆσαι. Holzinger accepts the LXX as the original. He also points out that χωροβατεῖν represents עבר in *v.* 9. The LXX probably gives the original in both places, and the M. T. here makes a double deviation which resembles the 'double omissions' elsewhere.

8. אלי ופה אשליך. Read with LXX A and many cursives ὧδε καὶ = אלי פה ואשליך. The Lyons Heptateuch has "redite huc

ad me," and this is the order of the Greek in 59. The Peshitta agrees with LXX A.

לכתב. LXX χωροβατῆσαι. כתבו, χωροβατήσατε. As this section in the Hebrew has plainly been revised (see below on *vv.* 6—10) it is probable that we have here two deliberate alterations. Perhaps the expression לעבר was not definite enough for the Hebrew reviser.

9. After בארץ LXX has καὶ εἴδοσαν αὐτήν = ויראוה.

אל המחנה שלה. Omit with LXX BA.

10 b. ויחלק שם. Omit with LXX BA.

2—10. This whole section exhibits marks of a Hebrew reviser. Take the passages which Dillmann himself criticises. In *v.* 9, where the LXX omits the words "to the camp at Shiloh," he says "possibly Shiloh is only a harmonistic insertion" and goes on to add "as also probably 8 b 'and here will I cast lots' where the emphatic front position of פה is striking." But in this latter passage the true text of LXX does not assign "the emphatic front position" to the word פה which causes Dillmann to suspect the clause, though strangely enough he overlooks this. And again the passage 10 b which he considers to have been deliberately omitted by the LXX is ascribed by him to the hand of a redactor. Surely if a clause considered to be due to a redactor is absent from LXX, it is quite possible that it was not in the text before the translator.

6—10. In these verses we have in the true text of LXX (1) the omission of פה in *v.* 6, (2) the transposition of אלי ופה into אלי פהו or פה אליו in *v.* 8, (3) the omission of "to the camp at Shiloh" in *v.* 9, (4) the omission of 10 b, all consistent with and supporting one another. The LXX plainly deserves the preference. See Intro., p. 7.

11. LXX insert πρῶτος = הגורל הראשון. But see Well. p. 128.

15. קרית יערים. LXX read בעל as in the preceding verse.

ימה ויצא. LXX B and Lucian εἰς Γασειν. A εἰς Γαιν: plainly reading a proper name. A reference to xv. 9 is not of much assistance, as ערי הר עפרון is corrupt. The second occurrence of ויצא in M. T. is plainly superfluous. LXX omit בן before Hinnom as M. T. does in the next clause.

16. בעמק. LXX and xv. 8 = בקצה עמק "the extreme end of the valley." Cf. ii. 18 a. τοῦ ὄρους has fallen out of B after μέρους.

17. For the second יצא LXX read עבר.

18. מול הערבה. LXX = בית הערבה which is generally accepted.

18—19. הערבתה: ועבר. LXX omit perhaps rightly, cf. xv. 6.

20. אתו. Omit with LXX.

28. גבעת וגו׳. LXX A and Lucian read καὶ Γαβααθ καὶ πόλις Ἰαριμ πόλις (πόλεις) = וגבעת וקרית ישרים ערים; omission by haplography in M. T.

B reads καὶ πόλεις καὶ Γαβαωθιαρειμ, πόλεις = וקרית וגבעת ישרים ערים, plainly a case of transposition. For LXX mistake of taking קריות as plural of קריה see xv. 24.

CHAPTER XIX.

In *vv.* 1, 17, 24, 32, 39, 40 the LXX give a very much shorter text, all these verses omitting למשפחתם.

1. למטה בני שמעון למשפחותם. It may be urged that the occurrence in the LXX of למשפחתם in six places (*vv.* 8, 10, 16, 23, 31, 48) would uphold the contention that the original Hebrew text had the expression in all twelve places (*vv.* 1, 8, 10, 16, 17, 23, 24, 31, 32, 39, 40, 48) and that the LXX had deliberately omitted the continual repetition of the phrase. But apart from the fact that this tendency of the LXX to deliberately omit is in dispute, it must be pointed out that this assumption of uniformity in the Hebrew is considerably weakened by the circumstance that in the M. T. as we have it *now* there is no uniformity in the use of the word מטה. It is found in the Hebrew in xviii. 11, xix. 1, 8, 23, 24, 31, 39, 40, 48, nine places, and is absent in xviii. 28, xix. 10, 16, 17, 32, five places. If there is no uniformity in the use of one technical term, why should there necessarily be uniformity in the use of another? מטה is rendered in LXX in xix. 8, 9, 23, 31, 39, 48, six places: *v.* 9 in the Hebrew does not contain it. Further in the subscriptions xviii. 28, xix. 8, 16, 23, 31, 39 and 48 LXX agree exactly with M. T. both in the longer and shorter forms; e.g. in xviii. 28 and xix. 16 where M. T. omits מטה. If in this inconsistent method of subscription LXX faithfully followed their text, we may assume that they generally did so in the introductory formulae; and that the differences are due to a Hebrew reviser who wished to make the superscriptions and subscriptions agree.

2. שבע. LXX שמע as in xv. 26.

7. עין רמון ועתר. LXX Ἐρεμμων καὶ Θαλχα καὶ Ἰεθερ = עיי רמון

and תכן (1 Chron. iv. 32), 'Ιεθερ is of course a doublet omitted in 54 and 75. Lyons Hept. Thaga.

8. וכל החצרים אשר. Omit with LXX. It is possibly due to dittography of preceding וחצריהן which may have been erroneously repeated and the phrase filled out by a subsequent scribe.

πορευομένων. The first two letters of באר were read by themselves.

9. LXX omits בני (1°) and inserts מטה before בני (2°).

10—12. שריד...משריד. LXX 'Εσεδεκ(γωλα) and Σεδδουκ plainly reading ד as the second letter. And as waw and yod were indistinguishable, modern scholars no doubt are right in reading שדוד: γωλα represents עלה in *v.* 11.

11. ופגע (2°). Omit with LXX. Repeated by M. T. owing to the preceding athnach.

13. המתאר. An old corruption, as is evidenced by LXX Αμαθαρ etc. All moderns read ותאר. LXX rightly Rimmonah.

14. אתו. Omit with LXX. As Dillmann points out, the construction is unusual and the gender wrong.

15 b. ערים שתים עשרה וחצריהן. Omit with LXX, as also the similar phrases in *vv.* 22, 30, 38 and 39. The words are rendered in LXX in *vv.* 6, 7, 16, 23, 31 and 48, and in the ten places where they occur in chap. xv.

16 b. הערים האלה וחצריהן. LXX has here and in 31 πόλεις καὶ αἱ κῶμαι αὐτῶν and in 48 αἱ πόλεις [αὐτῶν] καὶ αἱ κῶμαι αὐτῶν. In xiii. 23 and 28 M. T. has הערים וחצריהן. This corresponds to the true text of *v.* 48, which may have been that of 16 and 31.

27. בית העמק. LXX prefixes καὶ εἰσελεύσεται ὅρια, following which Steuernagel and Dr Driver insert והלך הגבול. As however הלך is only used once of boundaries in this book (xvii. 7) it is perhaps allowable to follow eight Greek MSS. mentioned in Holmes and Parsons and read ἐξελεύσεται. This would enable us to read ויצא in the Hebrew. Σαφθαιβαιθμε is perhaps a corruption of εἰς ἄφθαι Βαιθμεκ, ἄφθαι representing יפתח which came in from the preceding clause.

28. עברן. Peshitta עבדון, so all moderns.

29. עיר. LXX = עין which is generally accepted.

מחבל. Read מחלב. LXX ἀπὸ Λεβ = ἀπ' 'Ολεβ. Cf. Moore's critical note on Judges i. 31. אכזיבה. Insert ו with LXX.

30. ועמה. Read with all moderns ועכו according to LXX. For the ה = , cf. יריחה in 1 Kings xvi. 34.

33. ויהי (2°). LXX καὶ ἐγενήθησαν = ויהיו.

34. פגע. Read with LXX יפגע. So Dr Driver.

ביהודה. Omit with LXX.

41. עיר. Most moderns read with certain MSS. עין. The error is ancient; LXX πόλεις.

46. מי. Read with LXX מים and perhaps omit והרקון עם גבול מול. LXX did not understand this meaning of גבול (territory) and as elsewhere translates מול by πλησίον.

47, 48. Up till 1890—the date of Budde's *Richter und Samuel*—the extra verses in the LXX were regarded as an insertion from Judges i. 34, 35. But the opinion is now gaining ground that they were originally part of the Hebrew text, the ultimate source of both passages being "J." On the former side we have Hollenberg, Dillmann, Bennett and Steuernagel, on the latter Budde, Addis, Carpenter and Battersby, and Holzinger.

Assuming that the verses were in the original, the question must be asked whether any reason can be discovered for their omission by the Hebrew reviser? Holzinger suggests that the reason was the coincidence or correspondence (Übereinstimmung) with the passage in Judges. It is more probable however that the Hebrew reviser deliberately omitted that part of the narrative which recorded failure, and retained the part which recorded conquest. This would be naturally followed by the subscription.

On the other hand, if we take the view that the passages are insertions in the LXX, the difficulties in the way are considerable. First, what necessity was there for transposing the subscription? Second, why is the inserted passage, which is continuous in Judges, here divided into two parts, one part before *v.* 47 M. T. and the other after it? If the scribe had wished to insert Judges i. 34, 35 we should expect to find the LXX narrative parallel with M. T. up to the end of *v.* 47; then the insertion of the undivided passage, the whole being rounded off by the subscription.

As it is, the hypothesis of insertion requires us to believe that the LXX translator first transposed the subscription—a wholly unnecessary proceeding—that he then inserted the first part of Judges i. 34, 35, went on with M. T. and finally inserted the second part of the passage.

Now the only circumstances under which this is at all possible, would be in the case of a deliberate revision of the text: and if such has been the case here, all must admit that—with the exception of the transposition—it has been skilfully done. But is our translator a person capable of so delicate a piece of work? The other places where LXX revision is supposed to have taken place in this book, are in the accounts of the circumcision at Gilgal and of the circuit of Jericho, chapters v. and vi. Those who affirm that parts of these chapters are abbreviated from M. T. by our translator, will hardly maintain that the work has been done skilfully: so that, if the hypothesis of abbreviation there and of insertion here is to stand, we have to believe that the translator who did such clumsy work in chapters v. and vi. could perform a very skilful piece of work in chapter xix. On the other hand the hypothesis here maintained, that the LXX translator faithfully represented the Hebrew before him, avoids the improbability of supposing that clumsy and skilful work could proceed from one and the same source, and therefore has more claims to acceptance.

If Mr Thackeray's suggestion of two translators is accepted, the argument in the last paragraph would be partly invalidated; though a comparison with xviii. 4 should be nearly as decisive. But as pointed out in the Introduction, p. 16, another and perhaps a stronger argument is supplied for the faithfulness of LXX Joshua to its exemplar.

49. ויכלו לנחל. LXX ἐπορεύθησαν reading וילכו by metathesis. See the same mistake in *v.* 51.

CHAPTER XX.

It is generally admitted (not by Dillmann) that LXX gives in this chapter the more original text and that בלי דעת in *v.* 3 together with *vv.* 4, 5, 6 (with the exception of one clause) were not before the LXX translator.

7. ויקדשו. LXX καὶ διέστειλεν. Hollenberg suggests וַיַּקְרוּ, comparing Numb. xxxv. 11; an emendation which would be more likely if written וַיַּקְרְאוּ. The suggestion however has not met with acceptance as הקרה nowhere else has this meaning.

8. יריחו מזרחה. Not in LXX. Geographical addition.

CHAPTER XXI.

Mr Thackeray points out (*Gr. O. T. Gk*, p. 4) that in *vv.* 2—11 and 34—42 the word used in LXX for 'suburbs' is περισπόρια (17 times). In the rest of the chapter ἀφωρισμένα is used (35 times). He suspects Hexaplaric influence for the verses in which περισπόρια occurs, and suggests Aquila's version. But it should be noticed that περισπόρια is the word used in the corresponding sections of 1 Chron. vi.

4. הכהן מן הלוים. LXX τοῖς ἱερεῦσι τοῖς Λευίταις reading הכהנים הלוים. Comparison with *v.* 19, M. T. and LXX, where we get "the sons of Aaron, the priests," shows that the mention of the Levites is an insertion and הכהנים should be read. Cf. Lev. i. 5 etc.

5, 6. After הנותרים in *v.* 5 and גרשון in *v.* 6, LXX and Peshitta omit ממשפחת in both places. Dillmann, Bennett, and Dr Driver read למשפחתם. But the 'double omission' by LXX must be noticed, see Intro., p. 5.

7. LXX has κληρωτεί = בגורל rightly, cf. *vv.* 4, 5, 6 and 8.

9, 10. אשר יקרא אתהן בשם. Generally taken as corrupt. Steuernagel suggests ואת מגרשיהן. The LXX gives καὶ ἐπεκλήθησαν τοῖς υἱοῖς 'Ααρων, plainly reading ויקראו לבני אהרון. Comparison with xx. 7 suggests that וַיַּקְדִּשׁוּ which is there applied to cities may have been the word originally used here. When ויקדשו was read as ויקראו the other alterations had to be made in accordance. The sentence may originally have been "and they sanctified (them) to the sons of Aaron." For the omission of the acc. see Ges. Kautzsch 117 f.

11 a. אבי. Read with LXX אם.

13. הכהן. Not in LXX nor in M. T. *v.* 10. The three instances in the Hex. of the phrase "the sons of A. the priest" must all go. הכהן must be deleted here, and Lev. i. 7 (see LXX), and *v.* 4 above must run "the sons of A. the priests."

16. עין. LXX B 'Ασα = עשן, generally accepted.

18. עלמון. LXX B Γαμαλα. From 1 Chron. vi. 45 עלמת is generally read. Γαλαμαθ is found in several cursives.

20. ערי גורלם. LXX = ערי גבולם. Same mistake in *v.* 40. B has ἱερέων, a corruption of ὁρίων.

21. בהר אפרים. Not in LXX. Geographical addition.

25. גת רמון. LXX B Ἰεβαθα. Hollenberg points out that 1 Chron. vi. 55 gives בלעם which no doubt originally was יבלעם. He also notes that many Greek MSS read בית שאן and he is inclined to adopt it. Later scholars prefer יבלעם.

27. בעשתרה. LXX B Βοσοραν. Supposed to be shortened for בית ע׳. Steuernagel and Dr Driver read עשתרות.

29. עין גנים. LXX πηγὴν γραμμάτων = ספים which Hollenberg prefers, but he is not followed by other scholars.

32. חמת דאר. LXX omits דאר.

קרתן. LXX B καὶ Θεμμων; 1 Chron. vi. 61 קריתים. The καὶ before Θεμμων also represents the ק of the Hebrew word.

35. All scholars emend to רמון after 1 Chron. vi. 62. LXX omits the four words "Dimnah and her suburbs." Dr Driver quotes three Greek MSS as giving Ρεμμαν.

36, 37. All scholars insert the 20 words which are in the margin of M. T. They have however to be supplemented from the LXX by inserting at the beginning ומעבר לירדן יריחו and also after ממטה ראובן the words את עיר מקלט הרצח.

37. כל which is not in Peshitta or Vulgate is plainly an anticipation of the first word in the next verse. LXX reads πᾶσαι, no doubt a late insertion.

38. See on xv. 1.

40. תהיינה הערים האלה. Dillmann's explanation of these words "auch sollen diese Städte bestehen" makes them a command, but the sudden interjection of a command here seems very unlikely. LXX = "48 cities and their suburbs round about these cities; a city and its suburbs round about it, as regards (ל) all these cities." This may be right; if so the ל in לכל would be an instance of the generalising force of ל; a well-known usage of P (*Lex.* 514 b). The Hebrew reviser forgot this usage and inserted כן.

It is possible to argue that LXX did not know the exact force of תהיינה which, if correct, probably is "these cities *were to be*" (*Tenses* § 39), and that the exchange of this word for סביבות was thus facilitated. It is more likely however, that we have the work of a Hebrew reviser. Ehrlich suggests ותהיינה.

42 a, b, c in LXX is a repetition of xix. 49, 50. This repetition is important with reference to the question of revision. It is unfavourable to the general position of Dillmann, who affirms the work of a reviser was, to a considerable extent,

undertaken by the LXX translator. Any reviser skilful or otherwise would certainly have deleted one of the passages; and in point of fact that is what the Hebrew reviser did.

The repetition also negatives the suggestion of Holzinger (p. xv) that the LXX may have been subject to an independent revision. Holzinger's suggestion is important as betraying his feeling that the hypothesis of mere abbreviation will not account for the phenomena in the book.

42 d stands or falls with xxiv. 30 a. As mentioned in the Introduction, p. 9, there was a good reason for the Hebrew reviser dropping all reference to the circumcision at Gilgal.

45. "House of Israel." LXX 'sons'; rightly, as P ends at 42.

CHAPTER XXII.

2. ἀκηκόατε, misreading of שמרתם.

3. ושמרתם is difficult. If correct it cannot be rendered "but have kept," A.V., R.V. and others, but must be a modified imperative = keep therefore. But it is better to follow LXX with Steuernagel, Holzinger and Driver, who strike out the waw, and place the athnach at רבים, translating "up to this day ye have kept."

8. Dillmann admits the superiority of LXX here. With its aid we may restore as follows, making חלקו a Piel perf. introducing a circumstantial clause: "and with much riches they returned to their tents, even with very much cattle etc., having divided the spoil of their enemies with their brethren," i.e. the 9½ tribes:

בנכסים רבים שבו אל אהליהם ובמקנה רב מאד......חִלְּקוּ שלל וגו׳

Possibly the alteration arose from חִלְּקוּ being taken as an imperative Qal; שָׁבו was accordingly pointed שֻׁבוּ and ויאמר אליהם לאמר inserted. וישבו at the beginning of *v.* 9 which LXX omits was naturally added to carry on the narrative in a normal way. For a circumstantial clause ἀσυνδέτως defining *how* the preceding בנכסים רבים שבו was effected see Driver, 1 *Samuel* xxx. 2, where the same word is used.

The LXX had the same consonantal text as M. T. has after the inserted לאמר; καί in some Greek MSS. before διείλαντο is plainly an intrusion to ease the construction. With this unpointed text no scholar would think of vocalising otherwise than שָׁבו

and חָלְקוּ or חִלְּקוּ. No one would point the words as imperatives unless לאמר preceded, and even so the construction would be distinctly abnormal. Two imperatives separated from each other by a dozen words would be a very unusual construction in ordinary prose; 1 Sam. xv. 30 and xvii. 17 come nearest, and there the second imperative has waw copulative; Ruth iii. 13 is different. Normal Hebrew would require וחלקתם. The only alternative to a circumstantial clause is to read ויחלקו, but if that had been in the text one at least of the first two letters would have been retained.

11. אל מול. LXX, Lucian ἐφ' ὅριον = אל גבול. LXX did not know the word, or perhaps the meaning of אל עבר later on. But the passage is very difficult, see Driver's *Intro.* and Carpenter and Battersby.

12. "And the children of Israel heard." Omitted in LXX perhaps by homoioteleuton.

14. אלפי ישראל. LXX χιλίαρχοι as in 21. To judge from Numb. i. 16, this was apparently the traditional translation.

19. טמאה. LXX μικρά. Masius suggested μιαρά.

ואותנו אל תמרדו. LXX = וביהוה. The phrase was repeated, and ביהוה subsequently altered to ואותנו. מרד is always construed with ב except in Job xxiv. 13.

20. The last three words of the verse are troublesome. LXX does not represent לא, Peshitta read כלנו, Jerome read לו.

The interpretation generally given requires too much to be read into the words. We have to translate "So that though he was but one man, he did not perish (alone) on account of his iniquity." It is surely very doubtful whether לבדו can be 'understood' in this way.

It is possible that the text originally ran "And wrath came upon the whole congregation, and he himself perished on account of his iniquity," i.e. the result of Achan's trespass was two-fold—Wrath upon the people and destruction to the offender. So would it be in the present case.

But והוא גוע בעונו suffered interpolation previous to LXX by the insertion of אחד under the influence of Deut. xxiv. 16. How then did לא come in subsequent to LXX? It is most likely the gloss of a late Hebrew scribe or reviser who remembered the statement inserted in Joshua vii. 24 ff. that Achan's family perished with him. The text thus appears to have suffered two interpolations: one before and one after the LXX translation.

22. אל תושיענו. Holzinger's defence[1] of these words might hold good if we were dealing with dramatic poetry. In a plain prose narrative they are impossible.

The LXX had practically the same text as the Hebrew and gives a satisfactory sense; but as it paraphrases rendering ואם להעלות by ὥστε ἀναβιβάσαι, εἰ καί (B) or καὶ εἰ (A) before οἰκοδομήσαμεν may be an insertion and not represent ו or ואם before לבנות. ἐν ταύτῃ at the end of *v.* 22 and καὶ εἰ at the beginning of 23 may represent a transposition and misreading of היום הזה into בזה ואם.

We may perhaps emend אל תושיענו into אלהי ישראל, cf. *v.* 16 throughout, where מעלתם באלהי ישראל is used in the reproach of Phinehas whose words the two tribes seem to take up here. Then if we translate אם by a negative as after an oath we may translate "Not in rebellion and not in transgression against Jahveh the God of Israel was the building of an altar for ourselves." For ל introducing the subject see Isaiah x. 7 להשמיד בלבבו (Ox. *Lex.* p. 517 b), or it may be that the ל with infinitive belongs to the class of sentences treated of in Driver's *Tenses*, § 204. In course of time it was forgotten that אם had a negative force in the first part of the speech and it was taken in the same sense as ואם in the second part; then something corresponding to הוא יבקש was felt to be necessary.

Ehrlich's emendation of אל תושיענו into אלהינו עשינו is very close graphically: the metathesis of ע and ש could easily take place, and if we write אלתושענו by the side of אלהןעשנו the emendation seems almost self-evident. But the suggestion made above, that the tribes are taking up the words of Phinehas, seems preferable.

25. LXX omits "Ye sons of Reuben and sons of Gad." It looks like an intrusion.

27. Comparison of the Hebrew in *v.* 23 shows that ובזבחינו ובשלמינו should be ובזבחי שלמינו. This is upheld by the omission in A of ἐν ταῖς θυσίαις ἡμῶν. Cf. viii. 31 (D) where LXX is wrong.

28. καὶ ἀνὰ μέσον τῶν υἱῶν ἡμῶν. Probably a corrupt repetition of the previous expression or an amplification.

30. LXX omits "And the heads of the clans of Israel." As

[1] Die Erregung der falsch beschuldigten Stämme drückt 22 der anakoluthische Anfang der Antwort aus (auch תושיענו passt ganz gut in die sich überstürzenden Ansätze).

the chapter is from a priestly writer who would rejoice in repetition, the words may possibly have been in the text.

31 and 32. Omit with LXX "son of Eleazar" in both verses, as in *v.* 30.

33. καὶ ἐλάλησαν. This looks as if a later scribe read הדבר as וידבר.

34. The early omission of עֵד after למזבח in the Hebrew has caused considerable confusion in all the versions. The Syriac = ויקראו......למזבח אשר עשו עד כי עד וגו׳.

CHAPTER XXIII.

If the context is to be any guide at all *v.* 5 requires *v.* 4 to be confined to the nations still unconquered. The subject treated of is the fate of the nations that are left. Jehovah will drive them out and Israel shall inherit their possessions. The sentence וכל הגוים אשר הכרתי is out of harmony with the predominant thought; and in addition from a linguistic point of view is awkward and unsatisfactory: it may therefore well be a gloss. LXX however renders no help except for the insertion of יגבול before מבוא השמש. Jerome seems to have had a more confused text than even ours. The translation of בנחלה by ἐν τοῖς κλήροις shows that LXX did not understand the ב essentiae, see xiii. 6.

5. After יהדפם מפניכם insert from the LXX עד אשר יאבדו ושלח בם את חית השדה עד אשר ישמיד אותם ואת מלכיהם מפניכם. The omission according to Hollenberg (p. 18) is due to homoioteleuton; more probably it is the deliberate work of a Hebrew scribe, who summarised the omitted words by והוריש אתם מלפניכם. In xvi. 10 there is probably another instance of the omission of a large number of words and the insertion of a few words in their place. See note (3).

7. האלה אתכם. Omit at least האלה (2°) with LXX: *vv.* 7 and 12 display the hand of a reviser.

ולא תשביעו. Not in LXX, may have been omitted by accident.

9. ויורש. LXX B and Lucian give ἐξολοθρεύσει. A ἐξωλόθρευσε, Lyons Hept. exterminavit. As LXX give ἀνέστη and ἐδίωξε (see Driver's *Tenses*, § 30), which are quite inconsistent with the future, A has no doubt preserved the right reading.

ואתם. Not in LXX or Peshitta; to be omitted.

12. Omit with LXX ביתר and האלה (2°). אתכם omitted by LXX A. In view of *v.* 7, LXX A is to be preferred.

13. ולשטם. LXX ἥλους, rightly reading the plural ולשטים (confusion of ט and מ). But the translator did not know the meaning of the word, which occurs nowhere else in the Hexateuch.

14 b. הטובים. Omitted by LXX. הטוב in *v.* 15 shows that הטובים is required. The omission is accidental (homoioteleuton).

πάντα τὰ ἀνήκοντα. After ὑμᾶς had fallen out, corruption of the text took place; ἀνήκοντα occurs only once besides in the LXX, 1 Sam. xxvii. 8, and there it is inexplicable.

14 end. דבר אחד. Not in LXX, omitted perhaps as redundant.

16 b. וחרה etc. Omitted in LXX rightly. The clause is an exact reproduction of Deut. xi. 17. Its insertion arose from the Hebrew editor not perceiving that *v.* 16 a is the protasis of *v.* 15; otherwise *v.* 15 is an unconditional threat.

CHAPTER XXIV.

1. שכם. LXX Σηλω: repeated in *v.* 24. The alteration was made under the influence of the preceding notices of Shiloh, which is mentioned six times in the last few chapters. See Introduction, p. 8. Hollenberg however thinks it to be due to anti-Samaritan feeling.

3. כנען. LXX omits. The phrase 'land of Canaan' is priestly.

4. ואתן. LXX omits perhaps as unnecessary.

In accordance with LXX Hollenberg would add ויהיו שם לעם גדול ורב וחזק וירעו אתם המצרים. The above is Dr Driver's rendering of LXX. Hollenberg renders the third word by לגוי, the sixth by עצום, the eighth by להם. The omission could easily take place by homoioteleuton.

5. ואשלח את משה וגו'. Omitted in LXX. After the preceding clause had fallen out the Hebrew reviser felt the need of softening the abruptness of the transition.

כאשר must be altered at least to באשר. LXX B ἐν οἷς.

6. From this point LXX deviates into the third person and continues it up to the end of *v.* 13 no doubt from motives of reverence.

ואוציא את אבותיכם. LXX A ὑμᾶς. Dillmann and all later scholars take the mention of the 'fathers' here and further on to be due to the redactor.

אחרי אבותיכם. Read אחריכם in accordance with preceding note.

7. ויצעקו. LXX ἀνεβοήσαμεν. Dillmann and Bennett take the word as it stands as the *insertion* of a redactor: Steuernagel, Holzinger and Driver would emend to ותצעקו.

מאפל. LXX has νεφέλην καὶ γνόφον. Probably an amplification.

אל יהוה. Read אלי = to me, and see note on iv. 5. This emendation is independent of Steuernagel. It carries with it the emendation of וישם into ואשים and of ויבא into ואביא.

8. וילחמו אתכם. LXX B omits. In "I destroyed them" LXX read 2 pers. pl., confusion of ת and א.

9. LXX omits "son of Beor." Cf. xxii. 31 and 32.

10. ולא אביתי לשמע לבלעם. LXX καὶ οὐκ ἠθέλησεν Κύριος ὁ θεός σου ἀπολέσαι σε. Hollenberg suggests that לבלעם was taken for the infinitive of בלע to destroy. לשמע would then be omitted as unnecessary.

12. שני מלכי. LXX BA have "twelve kings," which is adopted by Hollenberg and all other scholars.

14 and 15. אשר עבדו אבתיכם. LXX τῶν πατέρων ἡμῶν (ὑμῶν) may be an abbreviation, or the Hebrew reviser may have objected, seeing that the phrase "God of our or your fathers" is frequently used of Jahveh, see Ex. iii. 13, 15, 16; Deut. i. 11, 21, iv. 1, vi. 3, xii. 1, xxvi. 7; Josh. xviii. 3? and cf. Acts iii. 13, v. 30, vii. 32.

15 end. LXX insert ὅτι ἅγιός ἐστιν.

17. αὐτὸς θεός ἐστιν. LXX did not understand the force of הוא in הוא המעלה. See ii. 11.

ואת אבתינו. Omit with 16, 44, 52 and Peshitta. See on *v.* 6.

מבית עבדים......האלה. LXX BA omits, and apparently Dillmann concurs.

18. את כל העמים. Shown by its position in the Greek after τὸν Ἀμορραῖον to be an addition to M. T. later than LXX and a subsequent insertion in LXX itself.

19. LXX omit אל perhaps as not necessary to the meaning.

20. אחרי אשר. LXX ἀνθ' ὧν = תחת אשר to be preferred as the more difficult reading.

22. ויאמרו עדים. Not in LXX BA. Not likely to have been omitted deliberately. It interrupts the speech.

24. LXX omits אלהינו rightly: it obscures the meaning "Jahveh (is the God whom) we will serve." See 21 b.

25. LXX continuing its alteration of Shechem into Shiloh adds "before the tabernacle of the God of Israel" on the basis of Ps. lxxviii. 60.

26. במקדש יהוה. LXX ἀπέναντι Κυρίου = פני יהוה, cf. v. 1; מקדש is priestly, and this passage is from E.

27 a. At the end of the first section Dr Driver inserts היום from LXX BA. This probably carries with it the insertion of באחרית הימים for ἐπ' ἐσχάτων ἡμέρων. Instead of פן LXX no doubt read כי which they translated by ἡνίκα ἄν. The phrase "when ye deny your God" may have been resented by the reviser who perhaps deleted באחרית הימים כי and substituted פן. Cf. xxiii. 16 a, "when ye transgress," etc.

30. After *v.* 30 LXX contains the interesting clause "there they put with him, into the tomb in which they buried him, the knives of stone with which he circumcised the children of Israel in Gilgal when he brought them up out of the land of Egypt, and there they are to this day." Cf. xxi. 42 d.

32. בני חמור. LXX omit בני. It is also omitted by LXX in the same phrase in Gen. xxxiii. 19. חמור was misread as אמרי.

32 b. יהיו לבני יוסף לנחלה. LXX A and Lucian have *καὶ ἔδωκεν αὐτὴν Ἰωσὴφ ἐν μερίδι.* B goes on immediately after ἕκατον, *καὶ ἐγένετο μετὰ ταῦτα κ.τ.λ.* = ויהי אחרי הדברים האלה ואלעזר בן אהרן מת. This was no doubt the original text. אחרי הדברים האלה was afterwards omitted and ליוסף לנחלה substituted. ויהי before ליוסף was either paraphrased by ἔδωκεν or misread as ויתן. בני is a still later insertion in M. T. The plural ויהיו is probably a textual error unless the word was actually put in the plural to refer to the bones. ὁ ἀρχιερεύς in B is an amplification.

After 33 the LXX gives an addition which may be rendered into Hebrew as follows:

33 a ביום ההוא לקחו את ארון יהוה וַיַּסֵּבּוּ בישראל וַיְכַהֵן פינחס תחת אלעזר
אביו עד מותו ויקבר בגבעה אשר לו 33 b וילכו בני ישראל איש אל מקומו
ואל עירו ויעבדו את עשתרת ואת אלהי העמים סביבתיהם 33 c ויתנם יהוה
ביד עגלון מלך מואב וימשל בם שמנה עשרה שנה

The originality of this passage is favoured by the ease with which it goes into Hebrew and by its fragmentary character.

Perhaps the verses were dropped out when the division into books took place. See Moore, *Judges*, p. 4, l. 24, for a similar conjecture in the case of that book; or there may have been objections to recording that the ark was carried about.